MULTICRITERIA DECISION-AID

MULTICRITERIA DECISION-AID

Philippe Vincke
Université Libre de Bruxelles

Translated from French by
Marjorie Gassner
Université Libre de Bruxelles

Foreword by
Bernard Roy
Université de Paris-Dauphine

JOHN WILEY & SONS
Chichester · New York · Brisbane · Toronto · Singapore

First published in French 1989. Copyright © 1989 by Éditions de l'Université de Bruxelles under the title *L'Aide Multicritère À La Décision*.

English language edition Copyright © 1992 by John Wiley & Sons Ltd,
                                                 Baffins Lane, Chichester,
                                               West Sussex PO19 1UD, England

Other Wiley Editorial Offices

John Wiley & Sons, Inc., 605 Third Avenue,
New York, NY 10158-0012, USA

Jacaranda Wiley Ltd, G.P.O. Box 859, Brisbane,
Queensland 4001, Australia

John Wiley & Sons (Canada) Ltd, 22 Worcester Road,
Rexdale, Ontario, M9W 1L1, Canada

John Wiley & Sons (SEA) Pte Ltd, 37 Jalan Pemimpin   #05-04,
Block B, Union Industrial Building, Singapore 2057

Library of Congress Cataloging-in-Publication Data:

Vincke, Philippe, *1951–*
    [Aide multicritère à la décision. English]
    Multicriteria decision-aid / Philippe Vincke : translated from
French by Marjorie Gassner : foreword by Bernard Roy.
      p. cm.
    Translation of: L'aide multicritère à la décision.
    Includes bibliographical references (p.) and index.
    ISBN 0-471-93184-5 (ppc)
    1. Decision-making—Mathematical models. 2. Operations research.
I. Title.
T57.6.V55   1992
658.4'033—dc20   91–30739
                                                               CIP

British Library Cataloguing in Publication Data:

A catalogue record for this book is
available from the British Library.

ISBN 0-471-93184-5

Phototypeset in 11/13 pt Times by Dobbie Typesetting Limited, Tavistock, Devon
Printed and bound in Great Britain by Biddles Ltd, Guildford and King's Lynn

To Annie, Lionel and Johanne

Contents

Foreword

This introduction to decision-aid undoubtedly fills a gap. Its objective, as described by the author (see introduction to the French edition) is: to write a textbook which, without going as far as B. Roy's book (*'Méthodologie multi-critère d'aide à la décision'*) would present students with basic concepts and methods more systematically and completely than Alain Schärlig's book (*'Décider sur plusieurs critères'*). This objective has been achieved and, indeed, even surpassed. The author's approach is didactic, but certainly not lacking in originality.

After a very interesting general introduction, which no reader should pass over, Philippe Vincke first tackles the modelling of potential actions which the decision process aims to carry out, or not. He then takes up the preference models on which decision-aid can be based. Next he reviews the key concepts of multicriteria decision-aid. The following three chapters are devoted to the three important families of methods which have come into being during the past twenty years or more and have been progressively developed and modified. From multiple attribute utility theory to interactive methods, along with methods involving outranking relations, quite a rich display is offered to the reader. The last chapter is undoubtedly the most original and stimulating one. The reader will discover some sources of reflection, some difficulties, pitfalls, important problems, but also some results and practical information. The book ends with an abundant, well-organized annotated bibliography.

The book is accessible to anyone interested in decision-aid (and even decision-making), be they student or practitioner. Philippe Vincke's clear, direct and concise style enables him to present a rather extended range of concepts and procedures in rigorous terms and in under 160 pages. No important aspect of the subject is omitted. This introduction to multicriteria decision-aid was the first of its kind to appear in French. Until now, it has had no equivalent in English.

I would draw the reader's attention to the title of the book: 'Multicriteria decision-aid', which means 'multicriteria aid for decisions' and which should be distinguished from 'aid for multicriteria decisions'. I take the opportunity given to me here to say that the expression 'multicriteria decision' is, in my opinion, not satisfactory. A decision, of course, relies in general on one or several criteria, but it seems quite difficult, in my eyes, to establish a clear distinction between decisions which would be multicriteria ones and others which would not. I am, therefore, delighted that, with this book, Philippe Vincke contributes to diffusing not only the term 'multicriteria decision-aid' but also everything the expression suggests.

As the author underlines in his book, using a single criterion to justify a decision offers an advantage: that of helping to state the problem correctly. However, this does not guarantee that the problem is well formulated with respect to reality. It simply means that the problem at hand is stated in such a way that the solution is determined entirely and solely by the formulation. It is, therefore, the way in which the problem is stated which creates the existence and the contents of the solution. The solution obtained cannot, under these conditions, depend upon the method of resolving the problem. Solving the problem consists of discovering what has been initially and implicitly built up by the way the problem was stated. It is possible, therefore, that for some readers, this advantage and its consequences will be considered indispensable to ensuring the scientific character of the thinking process. For those readers, monocriterion decision-aid necessarily appears to be more rigorous and more reliable than multicriteria decision-aid. We hope that this book will challenge their point of view.

As far as decision-aid is concerned, it may be advantageous not to separate the two stages of formulation and investigation. The multicriteria paradigm invites us to progress simultaneously on these two fronts. The results one obtains will then necessarily depend upon the process chosen to find them. Yet is it possible to do otherwise, since we are trying to fit into a decision process? Is it reasonable to accept the existence of ambiguities, of margins of error, of contradictory systems of logic and to want, at the same time, to dissociate the two thinking processes of formulation and resolution as we do when we seek to formulate what is usually called a well-stated problem?

Multicriteria decision-aid goes hand-in-glove with the search, not for truth, but for a mode of entry into a decision-making process in order to bring to it some enlightenment, some elements of answers to questions, whose formulation may be more or less confused and evolving. This explains the diversity of multicriteria procedures. It also helps us to understand why different procedures do not necessarily lead to giving exactly the same advice. With respect to our culture, this observation appears to be, if not altogether negative, at least disturbing. It does not reflect any kind of weakness in multicriteria decision-aid. It simply derives from the fact that the understanding one has of a decision-making process cannot be separated from the action one wishes to perform on it. That is why this book, like many others, does not deal with decision science, but with decision-aid science.

Bernard Roy
Université de Paris-Dauphine

General introduction

1. MULTICRITERIA DECISION-AID

Multicriteria decision-aid, often called 'analyse multicritère' in French and 'multiple criteria decision-making (MCDM)' or 'multiple criteria decision-aid (MCDA)' in English, is a field which has seen a considerable development during the last ten years. This phenomenon is illustrated as much by the increasing number of papers which have been published in journals devoted to operations research and decision theory as by the great number of communications given on the theme in scientific meetings. Several international working groups also meet on a regular basis to examine this subject (see section 3 of this introduction).

An encouraging feature of this development is the fact that it is not restricted to an isolated area, but concerns every branch of operations research. In other words, researchers and practitioners are more and more aware of the presence of multiple criteria in real-life problems of management and decision, whatever their nature.

As its name indicates, multicriteria decision-aid aims to give the decision-maker some tools in order to enable him to advance in solving a decision problem where several – often contradictory – points of view must be taken into account. The first fact which should be noted when dealing with this type of problem is that there does not exist, in general, any decision (solution, action) which is the best simultaneously from all points of view. Therefore, the word 'optimization' doesn't make any sense in such a context; in contrast to the classical techniques of operations research, multicriteria methods do not yield 'objectively best' solutions (such solutions don't exist). This is why the word 'aid' seems essential to us. The evolution of multicriteria methods illustrates this point of view perfectly: aggregation into a unique criterion (in order to bring the multicriterion problem back to an optimization problem) was contested and progressively replaced by more flexible, less mathematicized (some will say less rigorous) methods; similarly, interactivity has played an ever-increasing part in the proposed procedures.

Specialists in multicriteria decision-aid have made a habit of dividing

the methods into three great families, even if the boundaries between these families are, of course, rather fuzzy:
(1) multiple attribute utility theory,
(2) outranking methods,
(3) interactive methods.

B. Roy (1985) calls them respectively:

(1) unique synthesis criterion approach evacuating any incomparability,
(2) outranking synthesis approach, accepting incomparability,
(3) interactive local judgment approach with trial-error iterations,
while A. Schärlig (1985) talks about aggregation methods which are respectively complete, partial and local.

The first family, of American inspiration, consists in aggregating the different points of view into a unique function which must subsequently be optimized. The work related to this family studies the mathematical conditions of aggregation, the particular forms of the aggregating function and the construction methods.

The second family, of French inspiration, aims first to build a relation, called an outranking relation, which represents the decision-maker's strongly established preferences, given the information at hand. The latter relation is therefore, in general, neither complete nor transitive. The second step will consist in exploiting the outranking relation in order to help the decision-maker solve his problem.

The third and most recent family proposes methods which alternate calculation steps (yielding successive compromise solutions) and dialogue steps (sources of extra information on the decision-maker's preferences). Though they are mostly developed in the frame of multiple objective mathematical programming, some of these methods can be applied to more general cases.

Multicriteria decision-aid does not only encompass a family of techniques for the aggregation of given preferences on a given set. Preference modelling and defining the set of decisions are indispensable and delicate steps which, for the last couple of years, have been at the centre of some research.

Finally, one cannot ignore the links which exist between multicriteria decision-aid and other fields of research such as the theory of social choice, voting procedures, decision in a context of uncertainty, the theory of fuzzy sets, negotiation and expert systems.

We believe that multicriteria decision-aid will still see some important developments, on the theoretical side (the theory is still at its very beginning) as well as on the practical side, thanks to the increasingly user-friendly software which is currently being developed.

2. OUTLINE OF THE BOOK

The three first chapters present the basic elements of multicriteria decision-aid: the definition of actions (Chapter 1), preference modelling (Chapter 2) and the specifically multicriteria concepts (Chapter 3).

The set of actions is not, in general, an objective reality which imposes itself on the decision-maker and the scientist. Its definition is already part of the modelling process and can strongly condition the remainder of the procedure. It must therefore be clear that an identical problem may result in different presentations of the set of actions. In Chapter 1, we distinguish the case where the latter set is defined by listing its elements (as opposed to stating the properties which characterize them), is stable (as opposed to evolutive) and globalized (as opposed to fragmented) and we illustrate these concepts by giving some examples.

Although it makes up a whole field of study by itself, preference modelling is an indispensable step in decision-aid. In Chapter 2, we present the main models which are encountered in the literature to represent an individual's preferences according to some point of view: traditional models, models using one or two thresholds, those including incomparability, those including different degrees of preference, and those taking into account differences of preference or uncertainties. The mayor's problem, which ends the chapter, will allow the reader to test the relevance of these models to his own preferences on a particular case.

After defining 'criterion' and 'multicriteria problem', we recall, in Chapter 3, the main difficulty of this type of problem (which we already mentioned in section 1 of this introduction) and we introduce some specifically multicriteria concepts: dominance relation, efficient action, ideal point, nadir, substitution rate, preferential independence. These concepts are illustrated with numerical examples and some fundamental theorems for the determination of efficient actions are stated.

The three following chapters are devoted to the three great families mentioned in section 1 of this introduction: multiple attribute utility theory (Chapter 4), outranking methods (Chapter 5) and interactive methods (Chapter 6).

Multiple attribute utility theory has already been the subject of several didactic books: it therefore seemed useless to us to develop all of its aspects here. This is the reason why Chapter 4 is almost exclusively devoted to the most frequently encountered model, i.e. the additive model; we present its theoretical aspects, the direct construction methods, an indirect method (UTA), an interactive software based upon this additive model (PREFCALC) and an introduction to the analytic hierarchy process.

Outranking methods, to our best knowledge, have never been brought together in one text. In Chapter 5, we describe eight of the most representative or most commonly cited: the four ELECTRE methods, the MELCHIOR method, trichotomic segmentation, the PROMETHEE method and a recent outranking method including uncertainty.

Chapter 6 is, except for some details, a paper written with D. Vanderpooten and which appeared in *Mathematical and Computer Modelling* (1989). It contains the description of 10 interactive methods: even if most of them were originally proposed in the frame of multiple objective mathematical programming, we generalize the presentation whenever possible.

Chapter 7, entitled 'Miscellaneous questions' briefly goes back to a series of subjects which cannot be ignored if one is interested in multicriteria decision-aid. The first section examines some 'elementary' methods which we could have called 'natural' or 'naive': though they are quite simple to start, they may hide some traps which should be made clear beforehand. Intercriterion information, which is the main subject of section 2, is, in our opinion, an aspect which should, in the future, be the object of some intensive research; the latter information is indeed what differentiates one method from another and its thorough study will allow a better understanding of the implicit assumptions of each method; in section 2, we go into the concept of compensation, the problem of the interpretation and determination of the weights of the criteria and that of the independence between the criteria.

Sections 3, 4 and 5 of Chapter 7 are devoted to three fields which are strongly connected with multicriteria decision-aid: Arrow's theorem, voting procedures and choice functions. Multiple objective mathematical programming (a particular category of multicriteria problems) is reviewed in section 6. The following sections briefly examine multicriteria problems in graphs, taking risk into account, the use of fuzzy sets, negotiation-aid, software and expert systems for multicriteria decision-aid. Section 13 enumerates a list of references describing applications and sections 14 and 15 propose some routes for further research.

Finally, the bibliography includes a description of three books which we consider to be important, the list of references classified by author on the one hand, by chapter on the other and a list of keywords.

3. SOME PRACTICAL INFORMATION

Research activity in the field of multicriteria decision-aid is currently (1991) quite widespread: several international working groups have been formed and meet on a regular basis.

3.1. THE EUROPEAN 'AIDE MULTICRITÈRE À LA DÉCISION' WORKING GROUP

Founded in 1975, this group meets twice a year in some European city; working languages are French and English. A periodic bulletin (written in French) is sent to all members. To join the group, just write to

B. Roy
LAMSADE
Université Paris IX Dauphine
Place du Maréchal de Lattre de Tassigny
75775 Paris Cedex 16
France

3.2. THE INTERNATIONAL SOCIETY ON MCDM

This international group organizes on a regular basis, since 1982, a Congress on Multicriteria Decision Aid and publishes the *MCDM-Worldscan* bulletin (written in English), which includes a great deal of information about members, publications and scientific meetings. To join the group, just write to

R. Steuer
Dept. of Management Science
University of Georgia
Brooks Hall
Athens
Georgia 30602
USA

3.3. ESIGMA: EUROPEAN SUMMER INSTITUTE GROUP ON MULTICRITERIA ANALYSIS

Founded in 1985 by the participants of an intensive seminar on multicriteria decision-aid, this group meets once a year during the European Congresses on Operations Research. The working language is English and an information bulletin is published twice a year. To join the group, just write to

Ph. Vincke
U.L.B., C.P. 210
Boulevard du Triomphe
1050 Bruxelles
Belgium

To end, let us mention the regular organization of International Summer Schools on MCDA and the recent birth of *JMCDA* (*Journal of Multi-Criteria Decision-Analysis*) published by Wiley.

4. ACKNOWLEDGEMENTS

I would specially like to thank Marjorie Gassner who translated this book in record time: the quality of her work and her ever-present good humour make her a priceless collaborator.

My recognition also goes to Bernard Roy who wrote the foreword of this book and gave many judicious comments on its contents.

Finally, I would like to confirm my friendship for the members of the Aide multicritère à la décision and ESIGMA working groups, with whom I always enjoy working.

CHAPTER 1

The set of actions

1. INTRODUCTION

The definition of actions (solutions, decisions) is sometimes one of the most difficult steps of a decision-aid procedure. That particular stage is studied in detail and largely illustrated in a book by Roy (1985). In this chapter, we draw out the main definitions without going into all the nuances and variants they call for. Furthermore, it should be noted that very little research has been devoted to this important step of decision-aid procedures.

2. DEFINITIONS

The *set of actions*, denoted by A, is the set of objects, decisions, candidates, . . . to be explored during the decision procedure. It may be defined by:

- listing its members when it is finite and sufficiently small for an enumeration to be possible;
- stating the properties which characterize its elements when it is infinite or finite but too large for an enumeration to be possible.

Examples

- Ranking the 12 finalists of a music contest from best to worst: A is defined by listing its elements.
- Choosing where to build a new factory between 10 possible locations: A is defined by listing its elements.
- Choosing a circuit for a distribution round: A is the set of all Hamiltonian circuits of a graph.
- Assigning n workmen to n jobs: A is the set of permutations of n elements; it is also the set of all solutions of a system of linear equations with boolean variables.

- Determining the price of a commodity: A is an interval of the real line (even if, in fact, there are only a finite number of plausible prices, since the number of decimals is obviously limited).
- Solving a problem in econometrics: A is the set of solutions of a system of linear inequalities.

Given the complexity of decision-making problems, it is not always possible to define set A a priori. It may even happen that the definition of A is progressively elaborated during the course of the decision-aid procedure. Set A may therefore be:

- *stable:* it is defined a priori and is not open to change in the course of the procedure;
- *evolutive:* it can be modified during the course of the procedure, either because of intermediary results which appear during the process, or because the decision problem arises in a naturally changing environment (the two reasons can, of course, be simultaneous).

Finally, as will be made clear in following examples, it is interesting to distinguish between the cases where A is:

- *globalized:* each element of A excludes any other;
- *fragmented:* the decision procedure's results involve combinations of several elements of A.

3. IMPORTANT REMARK

Set A does not generally impose itself as an easily understandable objective reality. The decision problem can be modelled with the support of several different sets A, and the (stable or evolutive, globalized or fragmented) nature of the set depends upon the choice which is made. There is thus not one 'good' definition of A. Some definitions will lead to a more simple preference modelling but to a more arduous application of a decision-aid method, while others may have opposite characteristics. The definition of A does not only depend upon the problem to be solved and the actors involved in the decision procedure; it also strongly interacts with the steps that follow, i.e. defining criteria, modelling preferences, stating the problem and choosing the decision-aid method to be applied.

4. EXAMPLES

Example 1: localization of a new hydroelectric power station

A new powerhouse must be built in a given region; a preliminary study resulted in defining eight possible locations, amongst which the decision-maker must choose: set A is defined by listing its elements, it is stable and globalized.

Example 2: localization of two new hydroelectric power stations

In this case, the problem put to the decision-maker is to choose two sites amongst eight possible ones; the choice must be balanced and must not heavily favour any particular sub-region: the selection of one location thus strongly influences that of the second.

If A is defined as the set of the eight possible locations, then A is finite, can be defined by listing its members, and is stable and fragmented.

If, on the other hand, A is defined as the set of all 28 possible pairs of locations to be considered, then A is finite, can be defined by listing its elements, and is stable and globalized. In the latter case, the preferences and criteria which are built must obviously be applicable to pairs of locations rather than to locations themselves.

Example 3: choice of two candidates for two vacant positions

Two bank clerk positions are vacant in an important bank; the jobs are quite similar and demand similar qualifications. Twenty people have applied for the jobs.

Assuming both vacant jobs are independent and do not involve any collaboration between the two employees, set A, including the 20 applicants, is globalized.

On the other hand, if the two candidates who are selected have to work as a team, then the problem is similar to the one presented in Example 2 and set A is fragmented. Set A becomes globalized by considering it as the set of all 190 combinations of two candidates among 20.

Example 4: product-mix problem

A company manufactures plastic boards with properties of flexibility, resistance, weight, colour, . . . determined by customers. These properties depend upon amounts $x_1, x_2, \ldots, x_n$ of the different components used in manufacturing the plastic. A procedure must be set up in order to satisfy customers as far as possible.

In this case, A is the set of vectors $(x_1, x_2, \ldots, x_n)$ yielding a plastic which satisfies the requirements determined by the customers: it is infinite and can be described by the mathematical constraints which translate the physical and chemical properties of the mixture resulting from the components involved. A is an evolutive set because the constraints and the components of the mixture vary from one customer to another. Set A may also evolve for each customer if a preliminary study performed by the laboratory shows that the properties initially demanded by the customer are unrealistic or could be advantageously modified. A is globalized here.

Let us also note that when set A is defined in this way, it appears as a subset of a larger set (in this case $\mathbb{R}^n$).

Example 5: management of research projects

In a large company, a permanent committee must decide whether or not to continue current research projects and whether to accept or refuse new projects. Set A can be defined by listing its elements and is evolutive; it is fragmented because of eventual common aspects of several projects and because the total budget available is limited.

The interested reader will find the description and detailed analysis of 12 real-life problems and the related sets of actions in Roy (1985, ch. 3).

CHAPTER 2

Preference modelling

In this chapter, we state the main properties of preference models but do not prove them here: anyone interested in the proofs is referred to Doignon *et al.* (1986), Fishburn (1970a, 1985), Krantz *et al.* (1971), Luce *et al.* (1990), Monjardet (1978c), Roberts (1979), Roubens and Vincke (1985), Suppes *et al.* (1989), Vincke (1980b, 1988).

1. INTRODUCTION

Preferences are an essential element in the lives of individuals as well as communities. Their modelling is an indispensable step not only in decision-making, but also in economics, sociology, psychology, operations research, actuarial science, etc. In this chapter, we present the basic concepts which can be found in most of the research devoted to the ever-expanding field of preference modelling.

2. PREFERENCE STRUCTURE

We assume, to begin, that when a decision-maker must compare two actions a and b, he will react in one of the three following ways:

(1) preference for one of them,
(2) indifference between them,
(3) refusal or inability to compare them.

We write

aPb if a is preferred to b (bPa for the opposite),

aIb for indifference between the two,

aJb for incomparability.

Preference (P), *indifference* (I), and *incomparability* (J) relations are respectively the sets of ordered pairs (a,b) such that aPb, aIb, aJb. These are the three relations which can be found in most studies in preference modelling. They are defined on A, independently of whether A is globalized or fragmented.

In order for these relations to actually translate situations of preference, indifference and incomparability, it is natural (and accepted by all authors) to assume that they fulfil the following requirements:

$\forall a,b \in A$:

$$\begin{cases} aPb \Rightarrow b\not{P}a: \text{P is asymmetric,} \\ aIa \qquad : \text{I is reflexive,} \\ aIb \Rightarrow bIa : \text{I is symmetric,} \\ a\not{J}a \qquad : \text{J is irreflexive,} \\ aJb \Rightarrow bJa : \text{J is symmetric.} \end{cases}$$

Definition: the three relations {P,I,J} make up a *preference structure* on A if they satisfy the above conditions and if, given any two elements a,b of A, one and only one of the following properties is true: aPb, bPa, aIb, aJb.

3. CHARACTERISTIC RELATION OF A PREFERENCE STRUCTURE

Any preference structure can be completely characterized by giving the relation S defined by

$$aSb \text{ iff } aPb \text{ or } aIb \ (S = P \cup I).$$

Indeed, from the latter follows

$$aPb \text{ iff } aSb \text{ and } b\not{S}a,$$

$$aIb \text{ iff } aSb \text{ and } bSa,$$

$$aJb \text{ iff } a\not{S}b \text{ and } b\not{S}a.$$

Relation S is sometimes known as 'preference' as opposed to P, which is called 'strict preference'.

4. GRAPH OF A PREFERENCE STRUCTURE

We use the following graphic conventions for the representation of a preference structure.

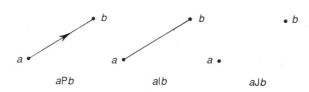

$$aPb \qquad aIb \qquad aJb$$

5. THE TRADITIONAL PREFERENCE STRUCTURE

The traditional approach consists in translating a decision problem into the optimization of some function g defined on A: this is the case in operations research, in actuarial science and in most economic models. The latter approach is equivalent to assuming that the decision-maker's preferences verify the following model (in the maximization case): $\forall\ a,b \in A$:

$$\left.\begin{array}{l} aPb \Leftrightarrow g(a) > g(b) \\[2mm] aIb \Leftrightarrow g(a) = g(b) \end{array}\right\}\ \text{the 'traditional model'.}$$

It can be easily verified that the underlying preference structure must satisfy the following conditions: $\forall\ a,b,c \in A$:

$$\left\{\begin{array}{l} aJb:\ J\ \text{is empty (no incomparability)}, \\[3mm] aPb\ \text{and}\ bPc \Rightarrow aPc:\ P\ \text{is transitive}, \\[3mm] aIb\ \text{and}\ bIc \Rightarrow aIc:\ I\ \text{is transitive}. \end{array}\right.$$

When the set A of actions is finite or countable, the latter conditions are also sufficient to ensure the existence of a function g fulfilling the 'traditional model'. When A is infinite, one must add some topological conditions which are generally satisfied in real-life applications.

Characteristic relation S associated with the traditional model verifies $\forall\ a,b,c \in A$:

$$\begin{cases} a\text{S}b \text{ or } b\text{S}a \text{ (non-exclusive disjunction): S is complete,} \\ \\ a\text{S}b \text{ and } b\text{S}c \Rightarrow a\text{S}c\text{: } S \text{ is transitive.} \end{cases}$$

The latter type of relation is called a *complete* (or *total*) *preorder*: it relates the type of situation in which the elements of A can be ranked from 'best' to 'worst' with eventual ties since

$$a\text{S}b \Leftrightarrow g(a) \geq g(b).$$

If there are no ties, then S is a *complete order*.

Definition: a preference structure is a *complete preorder structure* if it can be represented by the 'traditional model'; it becomes a *complete order structure* if the latter is true and I is limited to identical ordered pairs.

Comments

(1) In a complete preorder structure, I is an equivalence relation (reflexive, symmetric and transitive) and P is a 'weak order' (asymmetric and negatively transitive: $a\text{P}b$ and $b\text{P}c \Rightarrow a\text{P}c$); furthermore, the knowledge of P is enough to determine the structure entirely.
(2) In a complete order structure, P is a complete strict order.

6. TAKING INTO ACCOUNT AN INDIFFERENCE THRESHOLD

The transitivity of indifference, included in the traditional model, is incompatible with the existence of a sensibility threshold below which the decision-maker either does not sense the difference between two elements, or refuses to declare a preference for one or the other. This fact was already emphasized by H. Poincaré (1935, p. 69) and, before him, by some Greek philosophers, but it is D. Luce (1956) who first brought up this fundamental comment in the frame of preference modelling, illustrating it by the following example: if T_i represents a cup of tea containing i milligrams of sugar, it is obvious that no individual comparing cups of tea will sense a difference of one milligram $(T_i \text{I} T_{i+1}, \forall\ i)$, but will generally express a preference between a cup of tea with a lot of sugar and one with none ($T_N P T_0$ or $T_0 P T_N$, where N is sufficiently large); this contradicts transitivity of the indifference relation.

By introducing a positive threshold q, the model becomes: $\forall\ a,b \in A$:

$$\left\{\begin{array}{l} aPb \Leftrightarrow g(a) > g(b) + q \\[2mm] aIb \Leftrightarrow |g(a) - g(b)| \leq q \end{array}\right\} \text{the 'threshold model'.}$$

It can be easily shown that the underlying preference structure must obey the following conditions: $\forall\ a,b,c,d \in A$:

$$\left\{\begin{array}{l} aJb: \text{J is empty (no incomparability),} \\[2mm] aPb,\ bIc\ \text{and}\ cPd \Rightarrow aPd, \\[2mm] aPb,\ bPc\ \text{and}\ aId \Rightarrow dPc. \end{array}\right.$$

When the set A of actions is finite or countable, the latter conditions are also sufficient to ensure the existence of a function g and a threshold q satisfying the 'threshold model'. When A is infinite, topological conditions must be added; they are generally respected in real-life applications.

Characteristic relation S associated with the threshold model verifies: $\forall\ a,b,c,d \in A$:

$$\left\{\begin{array}{l} aSb\ \text{or}\ bSa: \text{S is complete,} \\[2mm] aSb\ \text{and}\ cSd \Rightarrow aSd\ \text{or}\ cSb: \text{S is a Ferrers relation,} \\[2mm] aSb,\ bSc \Rightarrow aSd\ \text{or}\ dSc: \text{S is semi-transitive.} \end{array}\right.$$

Definition: a preference structure is a *semiorder structure* if it can be represented by a 'threshold model'.

Comments

(1) In a semiorder structure, relation P remains transitive (to be checked as an exercise).
(2) Any semiorder structure can be associated with a complete preorder structure by defining

$$\begin{cases} aP'b \Leftrightarrow g(a) > g(b), \\ aI'b \Leftrightarrow g(a) = g(b). \end{cases}$$

It can be proven that

$$aP'b \text{ iff } \exists c: aPc \text{ and } cIb$$

$$\text{or } aIc \text{ and } cPb$$

$$\text{or } aPc \text{ and } cPb,$$

and I' is the complementary relation.

(3) From a graphical point of view, semiorders are characterized by the fact that the following configurations are forbidden (diagonals in any direction).

(4) A semiorder structure also has a very peculiar matrix representation, leading to the very interesting notion of 'minimal representation' (see Doignon, 1988b; Pirlot, 1990), which generalizes the notion of rank naturally associated with a complete order.

7. A VARIABLE INDIFFERENCE THRESHOLD

One drawback of the latter model is the fact that it takes into account only a constant threshold. Actually, many applications include variations of the indifference threshold along the chosen scale (a variation of $1000 doesn't mean the same when dealing with thousands of dollars or millions of dollars). It is thus often useful to introduce a variable indifference threshold such that, $\forall\ a,b \in A$:

$$\begin{cases} aPb \Leftrightarrow g(a) > g(b) + q(g(b)), \\ aIb \Leftrightarrow \begin{cases} g(a) \le g(b) + q(g(b)), \\ g(b) \le g(a) + q(g(a)). \end{cases} \end{cases} \text{ the 'variable threshold model'.}$$

Two cases may arise: if threshold function q obeys the following 'consistency condition': $\forall\ a,b \in A$:

$$g(a) > g(b) \Rightarrow g(a) + q(g(a)) \geq g(b) + q(g(b)),$$

then the underlying preference structure is that of a semiorder and, by transformation of functions g and q, the model can be brought back to a constant threshold one.

The latter situation occurs, for example, in the (frequent) case where the indifference threshold is given as a percentage of the considered value:

$$q(g(b)) = \alpha g(b) \qquad (\alpha > 0).$$

If function q doesn't obey the consistency condition, the preference structure underlying the variable threshold model must satisfy the following constraints:

$$\begin{cases} a\mathbf{J}b\text{: } J \text{ is empty (no incomparability),} \\ a\mathbf{P}b,\ b\mathbf{I}c,\ c\mathbf{P}d \Rightarrow a\mathbf{P}d. \end{cases}$$

When set A is finite or countable, the latter conditions are also sufficient to ensure the existence of two functions g and q verifying the 'variable threshold model'.

Characteristic relation S associated with this model is a complete Ferrers relation (cf. previous section).

Definition: a preference structure is an *interval order structure* if it can be represented by the 'variable threshold model'.

Comments

(1) Relation P is always transitive.
(2) Any interval order structure can be associated with two complete preorder structures by defining

$$\begin{cases} a\mathbf{P}'b \Leftrightarrow g(a) > g(b), \\ a\mathbf{I}'b \Leftrightarrow g(a) = g(b), \end{cases}$$

and

$$\begin{cases} a\mathbf{P}''b \Leftrightarrow g(a) + q(g(a)) > g(b) + q(g(b)), \\ a\mathbf{I}''b \Leftrightarrow g(a) + q(g(a)) = g(b) + q(g(b)). \end{cases}$$

These complete preorders are related to the rankings obtained by associating each action with the number of actions which are preferred to it and the number of actions it is preferred to (see Roubens and Vincke, 1985).

(3) From a graphical point of view, an interval order structure is characterized by the fact that the following configurations are forbidden (diagonals in any direction):

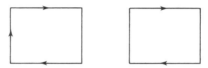

(4) An interval order structure also has a very peculiar matrix representation (see Roubens and Vincke, 1985).

(5) Interval order structures are closely related to the concepts of Guttmann scales, biorders, interval and comparability graphs and triangular graphs (see Doignon *et al.*, 1986; Fishburn, 1985; Golumbic, 1980; Roubens and Vincke, 1985).

8. COMPARING INTERVALS

The inaccuracy of measuring instruments (especially in decision problems) and the complexity of the decisions to be compared often make it difficult to translate the evaluation of a decision following some point of view into precise numbers. In such cases, each action a can be evaluated through an interval $[x_a, y_a]$. For the comparison of such intervals, two main types of situations have been studied in the literature.

(1) If it is necessary for two intervals to be non-intersecting in order for one to be preferred to the other, i.e. if

$$\begin{cases} aPb \Leftrightarrow x_a > y_b, \\ aIb \Leftrightarrow [x_a, y_a] \cap [x_b, y_b] \neq \varnothing, \end{cases}$$

then the preference structure is that of an interval order (in fact, this is where the name of the structure comes from): it is sufficient to let

$$\begin{cases} x_a = g(a), \\ y_a = g(a) + q(g(a)), \end{cases}$$

for the model to be brought back to a variable threshold one.

The interval order structure thus appears quite naturally when one must compare several decisions from a given point of view, their evaluations, from that point of view, being expressed as intervals. In the particular situation where all intervals are of the same length, the underlying preference structure is that of a semiorder (constant threshold).

(2) If one interval is preferred to the other as soon as the first is 'shifted away' from the second, i.e. if

$$\begin{cases} a\mathrm{P}b \Leftrightarrow x_a > x_b \text{ and } y_a > y_b, \\ a\mathrm{I}b \Leftrightarrow [x_a, y_a] \subset [x_b, y_b] \text{ or } [x_b, y_b] \subset [x_a, y_a], \end{cases}$$

then relation P is a partial order of dimension 2 and I is the complementary relation. A partial order of dimension 2 is, by definition, a transitive relation which can be seen as the intersection of two strict complete orders. In other words, it is the preference relation obtained when, comparing decisions according to two different points of view, it is possible to rank them from best to worst from each point of view, and a is globally preferred to b if a is before b in both rankings. In the situation we are concerned with here, the two rankings are respectively given by the order of the intervals' upper bounds and that of their lower bounds. We will come back to the concept of partial order in section 10.

9. TAKING INTO ACCOUNT INDIFFERENCE AND PREFERENCE THRESHOLDS

The practical use of the latter models obviously implies a phase of estimation of the indifference threshold. It may seem unrealistic to want to pinpoint a precise value above which there is strict preference and below which there is indifference. Real-life applications show that there is often an intermediary zone inside which the decision-maker hesitates between two different responses or gives contradictory answers depending upon the way questions are put to him. This observation led to the introduction of a preference model which explicitly includes two different thresholds: an indifference threshold, underneath which the decision-maker shows clear indifference and a preference threshold, above which the decision-maker is sure of strict preference:

$$
\left(
\begin{aligned}
&aPb \Leftrightarrow\ g(a) > g(b) + p(g(b)), \\
&aQb \Leftrightarrow\ g(b) + p(g(b)) \geq g(a) > g(b) + q(g(b)), \\
&aIb\ \ \Leftrightarrow\ \begin{cases} g(b) + q(g(b)) \geq g(a), \\ g(a) + q(g(a)) \geq g(b). \end{cases}
\end{aligned}
\right)
\quad
\begin{aligned}
&\text{the 'double threshold} \\
&\text{model'.}
\end{aligned}
$$

Relation Q, called 'weak preference' by Roy, translates the decision-maker's hesitation between indifference and preference (and not 'less strong' preference as its name might lead to believe).

The properties of relations P, Q, I involved in this model depend upon eventual 'consistency constraints' on the thresholds. Anyone interested should read Vincke (1980b, 1988).

In particular, let us recall the *pseudo-order structure* (Roy and Vincke, 1984b, 1987a) corresponding to a double threshold model upon which the following condition is imposed:

$$g(a) > g(b) \Leftrightarrow g(a) + q(g(a)) > g(b) + q(g(b))$$

$$\Leftrightarrow g(a) + p(g(a)) > g(b) + p(g(b)).$$

Let us note that a triple relation structure P, Q, I appears quite naturally when, comparing intervals as in section 8, the conclusion is

$$
\left\{
\begin{aligned}
&aPb \Leftrightarrow x_a > y_b, \\
&aQb \Leftrightarrow y_a > y_b > x_a > x_b, \\
&aIb\ \ \Leftrightarrow [x_a, y_a] \subset [x_b, y_b] \text{ or } [x_b, y_b] \subset [x_a, y_a].
\end{aligned}
\right.
$$

Characterization of the latter structure remains an open problem.

10. MODELS INCLUDING INCOMPARABILITY

In all the models presented up to now, relation J is empty, i.e. there is no incomparability. However, this is not a very realistic assumption since it often happens in decision-making procedures that one does not wish or is not able (because of lack of information) to compare two actions.

Incomparability appears even more frequently when contradictory opinions must be aggregated. Even if a decision is finally selected, it may be quite useful, during the decision-aid step, to put forward clearly any lack of comparison between actions. On the other hand, when, given the information available, two possible actions turn out to be incomparable, this helps decision-making since it amounts to putting forward some aspects of the problem at hand which deserve to be investigated.

There has been relatively little work done concerning models taking into account incomparability: we present here under the notions of partial order and partial preorder and we briefly recall the trial definitions of partial semiorders and partial interval orders. To these models must be added the concept of outranking relation which will be introduced in Chapter 5 and is more specifically linked with multicriteria problems.

10.1 PARTIAL ORDER STRUCTURE

A partial order arises when the elements of certain subsets of A can be ranked from 'best' to 'worst' without any ties. More precisely, we have the following definition:

Definition: a *partial order structure* is characterized by the fact that, $\forall\ a,b,c \in A$:

$$\begin{cases} a \neq b \Rightarrow a Vb \text{ (no ties)}, \\ \\ a\text{P}b \text{ and } b\text{P}c \Rightarrow a\text{P}c\colon \text{ P is transitive.} \end{cases}$$

In this case, a function g exists such that

$$a\text{P}b \Rightarrow g(a) > g(b),$$

all elements of A having different numerical values. (In fact, the necessary and sufficient condition for the existence of function g is that relation P must not include any circuit: the latter condition is obviously respected if P is transitive since the presence of a circuit implies that of an element a such that $a\text{P}a$, which is impossible.) The difference between this type of structure and a complete order thus lies in the fact that the numerical representation does not bring on a double implication, thereby authorizing incomparable pairs of actions.

Characteristic relation S associated with the latter model is such that, $\forall\ a,b,c \in A$:

$$\begin{cases} a\mathrm{S}a\colon \mathrm{S} \text{ is reflexive,} \\ a\mathrm{S}b \text{ and } b\mathrm{S}a \Rightarrow a = b\colon \mathrm{S} \text{ is antisymmetric,} \\ a\mathrm{S}b \text{ and } b\mathrm{S}c \Rightarrow a\mathrm{S}c\colon \mathrm{S} \text{ is transitive,} \end{cases}$$

i.e. S is a partial order.

Given a partial order structure, it is always possible to replace incomparabilities by preferences in a way which makes it into a complete order structure (Szpilrajn, 1930) and, furthermore, this can be done in at least two different ways. This fundamental result is at the basis of the notion of dimension of a partial order (Dushnik and Miller, 1941; Golumbic, 1980).

If several complete order structures are at hand on a set A, retaining only the preferences which are common to all of them yields a partial order structure: the latter situation will occur with the notion of dominance in Chapter 3.

10.2 PARTIAL PREORDER STRUCTURE

A partial preorder structure arises when the elements of certain subsets of A can be ranked from 'best' to 'worst' with eventual ties. More precisely, we have the following definition:

Definition: a *partial preorder structure* is characterized by the fact that, $\forall\ a,b,c \in A$:

$$\begin{cases} a\mathrm{P}b \text{ and } b\mathrm{P}c \Rightarrow a\mathrm{P}c\colon \mathrm{P} \text{ is transitive,} \\ a\mathrm{I}b \text{ and } b\mathrm{I}c \Rightarrow a\mathrm{I}c\colon \mathrm{I} \text{ is transitive,} \\ a\mathrm{P}b \text{ and } b\mathrm{I}c \Rightarrow a\mathrm{P}c, \\ a\mathrm{I}b \text{ and } b\mathrm{P}c \Rightarrow a\mathrm{P}c. \end{cases}$$

In this case, a function g exists such that

$$\begin{cases} a\mathrm{P}b \Rightarrow g(a) > g(b), \\ a\mathrm{I}b \Rightarrow g(a) = g(b). \end{cases}$$

Characteristic relation S associated with the latter model is a partial preorder (reflexive and transitive relation).

Given a partial preorder structure, it is always possible to replace incomparabilities by preferences in a way which makes it into a complete preorder structure.

If several complete preorder structures are at hand on a set A, retaining only the preferences and indifferences which are common to all of them yields a partial preorder structure.

10.3 PARTIAL SEMIORDER AND PARTIAL INTERVAL ORDER STRUCTURES

Both types of structures defined above are incompatible with the existence of an indifference threshold. It is therefore natural to try to define some kind of structure which simultaneously allows incomparabilities and intransitivity of indifference and will be called partial semiorder (when dealing with a constant threshold) or partial interval order (when the threshold is variable). Several definitions have recently been proposed in the literature, without any one really imposing itself up to now. Anyone interested should read Roubens and Vincke (1984a, 1985), Roy (1985) and Doignon (1988a).

11. SUMMARY OF THE MOST COMMONLY USED PREFERENCE STRUCTURES

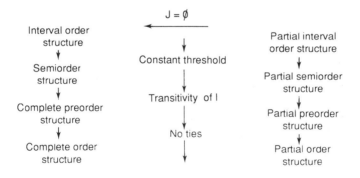

12. VALUED PREFERENCE STRUCTURES

In all the models described above, we assume that the underlying preference relation is unique in the sense that the decision-maker does not distinguish between 'strong or weak' preferences. If he does, it becomes necessary to assign to each ordered pair (a,b) of elements of A, a value $v(a,b)$ representing the 'strength' or the 'degree' of the preference. This is also the type of situation encountered when a and b are compared through some kind of voting procedure or survey in which some responses are in favour of a while others are in favour of b.

The properties enjoyed by the above-mentioned valued preferences can be quite diverse. Some of them are listed here:

$$
\begin{cases}
v(a,b) > 0 \Rightarrow v(b,a) = 0, \\
v(a,b) + v(b,a) = 1, \\
v(a,b) + v(b,a) \leq 1, \\
v(a,b) \geq \max_{c} \min \ [\,v(a,c),v(c,b)\,], \\[6pt]
\max \ [\,v(a,b),v(c,d)\,] \geq \min \ [\,v(a,d),v(c,b)\,], \\
\max \ [\,v(a,b),v(b,c)\,] \geq \min \ [\,v(a,d),v(d,c)\,], \\
v(a,c) = v(a,b) + v(b,c).
\end{cases}
$$

The first condition is a kind of antisymmetry: any preference of a over b excludes the opposite preference; the second is a probabilistic relation and is relevant, for example, in the voting case; the third can be seen as resulting from a vote including eventual abstentions; the fourth is one of the many ways of generalizing transitivity; the fifth generalizes the characteristic property of interval orders to valued relations; together with the sixth, it yields a 'valued semiorder'. The last property, i.e. additivity, leads to the concept of preference intensity and numerical representation models in which not only does $g(a)$ translate the value of a, but $g(b) - g(a)$ has a specific meaning: we will come back to this in the following section.

Many papers are devoted to the study of valued preference relations: they can be found mainly in journals concerned with either mathematical psychology or the theory of fuzzy sets. Anyone interested will find information in Fishburn (1970b, 1973), Doignon *et al.* (1986), Roubens and Vincke (1983a, 1984b, 1985), Doignon (1987).

In particular, given a (fuzzy) valued preference relation, one must choose what will be called strict preference, indifference and incomparability. Several different operators can be chosen for the definition of the latter concepts: one possible approach consists in defining a priori the properties that these operators must satisfy, then finding the class of operators obeying the imposed conditions: such is the trend of recent work by Ovchinnikov and Roubens (1991) and Fodor (1991).

13. COMPARING DIFFERENCES OF PREFERENCES

It may happen that the decision-maker is capable of comparing not only different actions, but also the differences of preferences between these actions. Given four actions a, b, c, d such that $a\mathrm{P}b$ and $c\mathrm{P}d$, one can sometimes get some extra information such as 'the preference of *a* over *b* is stronger, weaker, equivalent or incomparable with that of *c* over *d*'. The latter situation may lead to the definition of a preference structure on $A \times A$ completing the preference structure on A. The simultaneous study of both these structures and of the links between them is complex and, in spite of much research on the subject, is far from being finished. From here on in this book, we will only consider the 'traditional additive model', in which both preference structures are represented by a unique function g such that, $\forall \ a,b,c,d \in A$:

$$\begin{cases} a\mathrm{P}b \Leftrightarrow g(a) > g(b), \\ a\mathrm{I}b \Leftrightarrow g(a) = g(b), \\ [a,b] \ \rangle \ [c,d] \Leftrightarrow g(a) - g(b) > g(c) - g(d), \\ [a,b] \sim [c,d] \Leftrightarrow g(a) - g(b) = g(c) - g(d), \end{cases}$$

where $[a,b] \rangle [c,d]$ means that the preference of *a* over *b* is stronger than that of *c* over *d*, and $[a,b] \sim [c,d]$ means that they are equivalent. Obviously, the existence of such a function g implies very strong hypotheses on the preference structures (e.g. clearly, they must be complete preorder structures) and on the links between them. Many studies have already examined the latter problem and make up what is known as 'measurement theory': cf. Fishburn (1970a), Krantz *et al.* (1971), Roberts (1979), Roy (1985), Bouyssou and Vansnick (1988), Suppes *et al.* (1989), Luce *et al.* (1990).

14. PREFERENCE MODELLING FACED WITH UNCERTAINTY OR RISK

The main approach to the problem of preference modelling in a context of uncertainty or risk is the Von Neumann–Morgenstern (1967) theory of expected utility: given action a yielding consequence *x* with probability *p* and consequence *y* with probability $1 - p$, the 'value' of *a* is given by

$$g(a) = p \ U(x) + (1 - p) \ U(y),$$

where $U(x)$ and $U(y)$ are the 'values' respectively assigned to consequences *x* and *y* (in Chapter 4 we will describe some of the methods for obtaining these values). We are thus brought back to the traditional model since comparing actions becomes equivalent to comparing numbers, though what we are in fact dealing with are probability distributions. Other concepts have been introduced to deal with this situation: stochastic dominance, risk measuring, particular valued relations, and so on. The latter subject is covered by an abundant literature; see, for example, Fishburn (1982), Jaffray and Cohen (1982), McCord and De Neufville (1982), Cohen, Jaffray and Said (1983), Bouyssou (1984b), Colson (1985).

The example examined in section 18 illustrates how the expected utility model can be criticized (see also Allais, 1953).

15. GEOMETRICAL REPRESENTATION OF PREFERENCES

The development of computers has allowed great progress in the field of data analysis, in particular the use of statistical techniques such as factorial or discriminant analysis. Those techniques lead to geometrical representations, and thus to a visualization of the data at hand. They have also been adapted to cases in which the data concerns preferences (see Batteau *et al.*, 1981, for example).

16. GATHERING PREFERENCE DATA

Gathering preference data is an intricate problem: experiments have shown that the way one puts questions to a person may strongly influence his behaviour. Up to now, no clear general methodology has been developed; the development of user-friendly interactive software such as PREFCALC (cf. Chapter 4) may become quite useful in this respect.

17. ADJUSTMENT PROBLEMS

When a person is asked to compare objects (decisions, actions, candidates, . . .) two by two in terms of the three fundamental attitudes defined in section 2, one need not obtain one of the specific preference structures described in this chapter. It may be interesting, in such a case, to seek the minimal modifications which can be brought to the person's preference structure in order to obtain the desired properties. The problem is thus to adapt any preference structure with the aid of a specific structure, or to find the specific preference structure at a 'minimum distance' from any given structure; see, for example, Ribeill (1973), Vincke (1978b), Roubens and Vincke (1983b).

As an example, let us describe how one can determine the complete interval order structure $\{\hat{P}, \hat{I}\}$ which is at a minimum distance from any given preference structure $\{P, I\}$ (with no incomparability). Letting

$$v(a,b) = \begin{cases} 1 \text{ if } aPb, \\ 0 \text{ otherwise,} \end{cases}$$

$$\hat{v}(a,b) = \begin{cases} 1 \text{ if } a\hat{P}b, \\ 0 \text{ otherwise,} \end{cases}$$

the problem can be modelled as follows:

$$\begin{cases} \min \sum_a \sum_b |\hat{v}(a,b) - v(a,b)| \\ \hat{v}(a,a) = 0, \qquad \forall\ a, \\ \hat{v}(a,b) - \hat{v}(c,b) + \hat{v}(c,d) \le \hat{v}(a,d) + 1, \qquad \forall\ a,b,c,d, \\ \hat{v}(a,b) = 0 \text{ or } 1, \qquad \forall\ a,b, \end{cases}$$

which can be expressed as a linear program with boolean variables.

The function to be minimized represents a distance between the two structures of preference: the gap between indifference and preference is 1 while a reversal of preference has value 2. Of course, other conventions could be chosen.

The first constraint translates reflexivity of indifference, while the second reveals the following condition:

$$a\hat{P}b, \ c\hat{P}b, \ c\hat{P}d \Rightarrow a\hat{P}d$$

(implying asymmetry and transitivity of $\hat{P}$, along with the characteristic property of interval order structures).

Let us note here that it is essential with this type of problem to choose an adequate coding if one wants to avoid nonlinear mathematical programs.

18. EXERCISE: THE MAYOR'S PROBLEM
(cf. Vincke, 1981)

You are the mayor of a small town. During its next meeting, the town's council must choose one of four proposed projects a_1, a_2, a_3, a_4. Unemployment is a crucial issue: it concerns 12% of the town's 1500 working population. This is why the council has decided to make a financial effort in order to create new jobs. However, it has the right to reject all four projects (action a_5). Two major criteria must be taken into account while comparing the projects: the number of jobs that will be created and the cost of the operation. The former is dependent on outside events to which you assign certain probabilities. The table describes the evaluation of the different projects.

	a_1	a_2	a_3	a_4	a_5
Number of jobs created	50 or 10	110 or 10	50	110 or 10	0
Corresponding probabilities	p $1-p$	$p/2$ $1-p/2$	1	1/2 1/2	1
Cost	c	c	$2c$	$2c$	0

In this table $p \approx 0.1$ and c is approximately 10% of the town's annual income.

● *First question:* for each of the 10 pairs of actions, point out which of the following statements best reflects your opinion, given the information available:

$a_i P a_j$: 'without any hestiation, I prefer a_i to a_j',

$a_i I a_j$: 'I am indifferent between a_i and a_j',

$a_i Q a_j$: 'a_j is definitely not better than a_i, but I cannot make up my mind between $a_i P a_j$ and $a_i I a_j$',

$a_i J a_j$: 'I cannot compare a_i and a_j'.

● *Second question:* same as the first, but taking into account only the first criterion (number of jobs created and corresponding probabilities).

You can answer 'no' to the following questions. If you answer 'yes', give the required evaluation any way you choose to (precise number, interval, sentence, . . .).

● *Third question:* can you evaluate probability π_1, such that, in your opinion, getting 110 new jobs with probability π_1 or 10 jobs with probability $1 - \pi_1$ is equivalent to being certain of getting 50 new jobs?

● *Fourth question:* given that an investment of $2c$ ensures the creation of 50 new jobs, can you give a minimum number of job creations that an investment of c should ensure?

● *Fifth question:* can you evaluate the probability π_2 such that, in your opinion, getting 110 new jobs with probability π_2 or 10 jobs with probability $1 - \pi_2$ is equivalent to getting 50 jobs with probability 0.1 or 10 jobs with probability 0.9?

● *Sixth question:* can you compare the difference between 10 and 50 jobs with that between 50 and 110 jobs?

You are asked to answer these questions before reading the rest of this section; if you have the opportunity, put the problem to your students, family and colleagues.

In 1980, this set of questions was given to about 300 students, researchers and teachers in management, economics and operations research in France, Belgium and Switzerland. We summarize here the results we obtained in order for you to compare them with your own conclusions. From here on, in this section,

$$\begin{cases} a \rangle b \text{ means } aPb \text{ or } aQb, \\ a \sim b \text{ means } aIb \text{ or } aJb, \\ \text{all numbers are percentages.} \end{cases}$$

The three first tables concern questions 1 and 2.

Table 1 gives the percentages of answers in which all comparisons were expressed by strict preferences (column P), strict preferences and indifferences (column P, I), strict preferences, indifferences and weak preferences (column P, I, Q).

Table 2 gives, for relations P, $\rangle$ and I, the percentages of answers in which these relations include intransitivities. These percentages concern the answers including at least one triple $\{a_i,a_j,a_k\}$ of actions such that a_iPa_j and a_jPa_k (resp. $\rangle$ and I).

Table 3 gives the percentages of answers in which the ordered pairs of relations (P,I), ($\rangle$,I) and ($\rangle$, $\sim$) have interval order (i.o.), semiorder (s.o.) and complete preorder (c.p.) structures along with the percentages of answers having a pseudo-order (ps.o.) structure.

Table 1	P	P,I	P,I,Q
1st question	14.75	22.66	70.50
2nd question	33.81	53.95	88.84

Table 2	Intransitivities of P	Intransitivities of $\rangle$	Intransitivities of I
1st question	45.69	49.09	22.41
2nd question	18.30	20.57	9.97

Table 3	(P,I)			($\rangle$,I)			($\rangle$, $\sim$)			(P,I,Q)
	i.o.	s.o.	c.p.	i.o.	s.o.	c.p.	i.o.	s.o.	c.p.	ps.o.
1st question	14.74	14.74	14.38	39.92	39.92	38.12	50.35	47.84	42.80	24.82
2nd question	44.96	44.96	44.24	73.38	73.38	72.66	79.13	77.69	75.53	66.90

Table 4 concerns the compatibility of the answers received to the second question with the 'expected utility model' (cf. section 14). When applied to this example, the latter model yields:

$$\begin{cases} g(a_1) = p \ U(50) + (1-p) \ U(10), \\ g(a_2) = p/2 \ U(110) + (1-p/2) \ U(10), \\ g(a_3) = U(50), \\ g(a_4) = \tfrac{1}{2} \ U(110) + \tfrac{1}{2} \ U(10), \\ g(a_5) = U(0). \end{cases}$$

As a result, any set of preferences will not necessarily be compatible with the expected utility model. For example, we have

$$g(a_1) > g(a_2) \Rightarrow p\ U(50) > p/2\ U(110) + p/2\ U(10)$$

$$\Rightarrow U(50) > \tfrac{1}{2}\ U(110) + \tfrac{1}{2}\ U(10)$$

$$\Rightarrow g(a_3) > g(a_4).$$

Table 4 shows the percentages of answers in which ordered pairs of relations (P,I), $(\rangle,I)$ and $(\rangle, \sim)$ are compatible with the expected utility model.

Table 4	(P,I)	$(\rangle,I)$	$(\rangle, \sim)$
2nd question	14.74	23.38	23.38

Table 5 summarizes the types of answers received to questions 3 to 6.

Table 5	Absence of answer	'no' answers	Literary answers	Answers given by		
				bounds	intervals	precise numbers
3rd question	0.02	0.20	0.08	0.12	0.17	0.41
4th question	0.02	0.06	0.05	0.15	0.25	0.47
5th question	0.07	0.23	0.07	0.06	0.07	0.50
6th question	0.16	0.43	0.23	Made comparisons 0.18		

Actions a_1 and a_2 have identical costs: once could thus expect identical answers to that pair of actions. In fact, 32.73% of the answers were different and 12.95% included a reversal of preference. The same is true for a_3 and a_4, for which 46.4% of the answers were different and 17.62% included a reversal of preference.

For people having given a precise number as an answer to the third question, the expected utility model yields

$$\pi_1\ U(110) + (1 - \pi_1)\ U(10) = U(50).$$

For each value of π_1, for the second question, one obtains a complete preorder compatible with that value: 14% of the people who proposed a precise value for π_1 gave, for the second question, a complete preorder compatible with that value. Similarly, 13% of the people who proposed a precise value for π_2 (fifth question) gave, for the second question, a complete preorder compatible with that value. Finally, 6% of the people who made the comparison proposed in the sixth question, gave, for the second question, a complete preorder compatible with their answer.

CHAPTER 3

The basic concepts of multicriteria decision-aid

1. CRITERION AND CONSISTENT FAMILY OF CRITERIA

We define a *criterion* as a function g, defined on A, taking its values in a totally ordered set, and representing the decision-maker's preferences according to some point of view. It will be called:

a *true criterion* if the underlying preference structure is a complete preorder structure ('traditional model');
a *semi-criterion* if the underlying preference structure is a semiorder structure ('threshold model');
an *interval criterion* if the underlying preference structure is an interval order structure ('variable threshold model');
a *pseudo-criterion* if the underlying preference structure is a pseudo-order structure ('double-threshold model', with constraints on the thresholds).

When the problem at hand includes the consideration of several criteria, they will be noted g_1, g_2,...,g_j,...,g_n: from here on, we will use the terms criterion g_j or criterion j interchangeably. The evaluation of action a according to criterion j is written $g_j(a)$.

The respresentation of different points of view (aspects, factors, characteristics) with the help of a family $F=\{g_1,...,g_j,...,g_n\}$ of criteria is undoubtedly the most delicate part of the decision problem's formulation (cf. Bouyssou, 1990). Up to now, only B. Roy (1985) has proposed a methodology leading to the definition of F and analysing the different types of problems that may occur: we strongly recommend this work for relevant details. If possible, family F of criteria should represent all the different aspects of the problem at hand while avoiding redundancies: Roy and Bouyssou (1987b) give a definition of what they call a *consistent family of criteria* along with the operational tests allowing to check if a family of criteria is consistent.

Convention: except if otherwise mentioned, we assume that preferences increase with the g_j's.

2. MULTICRITERIA PROBLEM

Definition: a *multicriteria decision problem* is a situation in which, having defined a set A of actions and a consistent family F of criteria on A, one wishes

(1) to determine a subset of actions considered to be the best with respect to F (choice problem),
(2) to divide A into subsets according to some norms (sorting problem), or
(3) to rank the actions of A from best to worst (ranking problem).

A multicriteria decision problem is obviously not an objective reality which can be given an immediate description accepted by everyone (as are usually phenomena pertaining to 'exact sciences'). The definition given above should rather be seen as a way to formulate a multicriteria decision problem. It will in fact frequently happen that a real-life problem gives rise to a mixture of choice, sorting and ranking problems. It is also important to note that a same real-life problem may imply:

• different definitions of A,
• different definitions of F,
• different statements of the problem (choice, sorting or ranking).

The latter remark is perfectly illustrated by the 12 real-life examples which are analysed by Roy all through his book (1985).

3. MULTIPLE OBJECTIVE MATHEMATICAL PROGRAM

Definition: a *multiple objective mathematical program* is a problem which aims to find a vector $x \in \mathbb{R}^p$ satisfying constraints of the type

$$h_i(x) \leq 0, \qquad i = 1, 2, \ldots, m,$$

obeying eventual integrality conditions and maximizing functions

$$g_j(x), \qquad n = 1,2,\ldots,n.$$

A multiple objective mathematical program is thus in fact a multicriteria decision problem in which

- $A = \{x : h_i(x) \leq 0, \ \forall \ i\} \subset \mathbb{R}^p,$
- $F = \{g_1(x),\ldots,g_n(x)\}$ is a family of true criteria,
- one aims to find a 'best' action (choice problem).

A multiple objective mathematical program is said to be *linear* if functions h_i $(i = 1,2,\ldots,m)$ and g_j $(j = 1,2,\ldots,n)$ depend linearly on x:

$$\begin{cases} \max \ C^j x, & j = 1,2,\ldots,n, \\ Dx \leq b, \\ x \geq 0, \end{cases}$$

where C^j, D and b are matrices of respective dimensions $1 \times p$, $m \times p$ and $m \times 1$.

4. DIFFICULTY OF MULTICRITERIA PROBLEMS

The main difficulty in a multicriteria problem lies in the fact that it is an ill-defined mathematical problem, i.e. it has no objective solution. There is generally no action which is better than all the others for all the criteria considered simultaneously: therefore, the concept of optimal solution doesn't make any sense in a multicriteria context. Similarly, a ranking problem will result in an objective solution only if all the criteria considered yield the same ranking, which is obviously exceptional.

'Solving' a multicriteria decision problem is therefore not searching for some kind of hidden truth (though this is the case when dealing with classical optimization problems), but rather helping the decision-maker to master the (often complex) data involved in his problem and advance toward a solution (cf. Roy, 1990a). The latter will thus be a 'compromise action' and it must be emphasized that it depends strongly on the decision-maker's personality, on the circumstances in which the decision-aiding process takes place, on the way in which the problem is presented and on the method which is used. These characteristics are, of course, quite embarrassing for scientific researchers who are used to solving problems in which the solutions exist 'independently of themselves'. It is undeniable that part of the scientific community still considers that multicriteria decision-aid is not serious or not very rigorous. We will also see that, in some of the methods which have been proposed, many researchers have tried to bring multicriteria decision problems back to well-defined mathematical problems, thereby risking to completely deform them.

However, the fact that most decision problems do involve several criteria seems to be widely acknowledged nowadays. As often happens in applied mathematics, the development of multicriteria decision-aid was dictated by real-life problems. It is therefore not surprising that methods have appeared in a rather diffuse way, without any clear general methodology or basic theory. The gap is being progressively filled by recent research.

5. DOMINANCE RELATION

Definition: given two elements a and b of A, a *dominates* b (aDb) iff

$$g_j(a) \geq g_j(b), \qquad j = 1, 2, \ldots, n,$$

where at least one of the inequalities is strict.

The reader can check, as an exercise, that the dominance relation is a strict partial order (asymmetric and transitive relation). Clearly, dominance of a over b translates a sort of unanimity of points of view in favour of a. It is also obvious that the dominance relation is generally quite poor (very few pairs of actions verify it), if not empty (no pair of actions verifies it).

6. EFFICIENT ACTION

Definition: action a is efficient iff no action of A dominates it.

The set of efficient actions (which can be A when the dominance relation is empty) is generally considered as the set of the only interesting actions, even if there are sometimes good reasons for not definitively rejecting non-efficient actions. This is why a great deal of authors have searched for characterizations and methods to determine such actions: we will give some examples of this later.

Finally, it is important to note that the definition of an efficient action gave rise to some variations, leading to the concepts of weak efficiency, strong efficiency, proper efficiency, and so on (Geoffrion, 1968; Steuer, 1986; Henig, 1990).

7. THE IMAGE OF A IN THE CRITERIA SPACE

Since a criterion is a function g taking its values in a totally ordered set, $g_j(a)$ can always be represented by a real number.

The set of evaluations of a given action a, $\{g_1(a),...,g_n(a)\}$, can thus be represented by a point in $\mathbb{R}^n$.

Definition: the *image* of A in the criteria space is the set Z_A of points in $\mathbb{R}^n$ one obtains when each action a is represented by the point whose coordinates are $(g_1(a),...,g_n(a))$.

8. IDEAL POINT

Definition: the *ideal point*, in $\mathbb{R}^n$, is the point whose coordinates are $(z_1^*,...,z_n^*)$, where

$$z_j^* = \max_A g_j(a), \qquad j = 1,2,...,n.$$

We will denote by $\hat{a}^j$ the action which is best according to criterion j:

$$g_j(\hat{a}^j) = z_j^*$$

(there may be several).

9. PAYOFF MATRIX

Definition: the payoff matrix is the matrix G $(n \times n)$ defined by

$$G_{kl} = g_k(\hat{a}^l), \qquad k,l = 1,2,...,n.$$

It is thus the matrix containing, for each action $\hat{a}^l$, its evaluations according to all the criteria; in particular,

$$G_{ll} = z_l^*,$$

the ideal point's components can be read on the diagonal of the payoff matrix. It should be noted that the payoff matrix is unique only if each criterion reaches its maximum at only one action.

10. THE NADIR

Definition: the *nadir* is the point whose coordinates are $(\underline{z}_1, \ldots, \underline{z}_n)$ where

$$\underline{z}_j = \min_l G_{jl}, \qquad j = 1, 2, \ldots, n.$$

It obviously depends upon the chosen payoff matrix and set A.

11. SOME NUMERICAL EXAMPLES

The following two examples illustrate the concepts introduced above.

(1) A consumer wants to buy a television set and, after a first selection, retains eight models and then evaluates them by taking into account the price, quality of picture, quality of sound and maintenance contract (V.G. = very good, G. = good, A. = average, N.G. = not good).

Remark: in order to respect the convention of section 1, we have modified the price criterion by changing signs, thereby getting a maximization problem.

Model	− Price	Picture quality	Sound quality	Maintenance contract
T1	− 1300	V.G.	V.G.	A.
T2	− 1200	V.G.	V.G.	G.
T3	− 1150	V.G.	G.	G.
T4	− 1000	G.	G.	N.G.
T5	− 950	G.	G.	A.
T6	− 950	A.	G.	N.G.
T7	− 900	G.	A.	N.G.
T8	− 900	A.	A.	A.

The dominance relation can be represented by the accompanying graph:

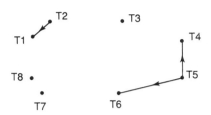

(Note that if there were an indifference threshold of 50 on the prices, one could be tempted to say that T2 dominates T3.)

The efficient actions are T2, T3, T5, T7 and T8.

The image of A in the criteria space is the set of points $(-1300,2,2,0)$, $(-1200,2,2,1)$, $(-1150,2,1,1)$, $(-1000,1,1,-1)$, $(-950,1,1,0)$, $(-950,0,1,-1)$, $(-900,1,0,-1)$, $(-900,0,0,0)$ in $\mathbb{R}^4$ (V.G. was somewhat arbitrarily replaced by 2, G. by 1, A. by 0 and N.G. by -1). The ideal point (with our coding) is $(-900,2,2,1)$.

Payoff matrix: because of the number of ties, many payoff matrices can be considered. We give one here as an example.

	− Price	Picture quality	Sound quality	Maintenance contract
$\hat{a}^1 = T8$	− 900	0	0	0
$\hat{a}^2 = T2$	− 1200	2	2	1
$\hat{a}^3 = T2$	− 1200	2	2	1
$\hat{a}^4 = T3$	− 1150	2	1	1

The nadir, for this payoff matrix, is $(-1200,0,0,0)$.

(2) Consider the following bi-objective linear program:

$$\begin{cases} x_1 + 2x_2 \leq 16 \\ x_1 + x_2 \leq 9 \\ x_1 - x_2 \leq 6 \\ x_1, \ x_2 \geq 0 \end{cases}$$

$$\max g_1(x_1, x_2), \text{ where } g_1(x_1, x_2) = x_1,$$

$$\max g_2(x_1, x_2), \text{ where } g_2(x_1, x_2) = x_1 + 3x_2.$$

The set of actions is, in this case, the polygon of $\mathbb{R}^2$ represented here.

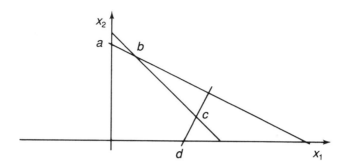

The image of A in the criteria space is represented here.

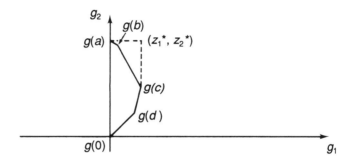

The efficient actions are the actions with images making up segments $[g(a), g(b)]$ and $[g(b), g(c)]$, i.e. segments $[a, b]$ and $[b, c]$. All other actions are dominated by at least one of them.

The ideal point is $(z_1^*, z_2^*) = (7.5, 24)$.

The payoff matrix is, this time, unique:

	g_1	g_2
$\hat{a}^1 = c$	7.5	12
$\hat{a}^2 = a$	0	24

The nadir is point $(0, 12)$.

12. SOME THEOREMS

Theorem 1: if $\bar{a}$ is an action which maximizes, in A,

$$\sum_{j=1}^{n} \lambda_j g_j(a),$$

where $\lambda_j > 0$, $\forall j$, then $\bar{a}$ is efficient.
(The converse of this theorem is true only under certain convexity assumptions on Z_A.)

Theorem 2: if $\bar{a}$ is the unique action in A which minimizes the following amount (known as the *weighted distance of Tchebychev*)

$$\max_j \lambda_j(z_j^{**} - g_j(a)),$$

where $\lambda_j > 0$ and $z_j^{**} > z_j^*$, $\forall j$, then $\bar{a}$ is efficient and conversely. If $\bar{a}$ is not unique, at least one of the optimal actions is efficient.

Theorem 3: if $\bar{a}$ minimizes, in A, the following amount (known as the *augmented weighted distance of Tchebychev*)

$$\max_j \lambda_j(z_j^{**} - g(a)) - \sum_{j=1}^{n} \rho_j g_j(a),$$

where $\lambda_j > 0$, $z_j^{**} > z_j^*$ and $\rho_j > 0$ is arbitrarily small, then $\bar{a}$ is efficient and conversely.

Theorem 1 shows that the optimization of a positive linear combination of criteria always yields an efficient action. Theorems 2 and 3 allow efficient actions to be characterized as those which minimize a sort of distance to a point which slightly dominates the ideal point.

13. DETERMINATION OF EFFICIENT ACTIONS

The previous theorems show that the determination of efficient actions is achieved through solving parametric optimization problems. Several authors have proposed procedures allowing those solutions to be generated or to check whether an action is efficient or not, when A is defined by stating properties characterizing its elements. Anyone interested will find extra information in Chalmet *et al.* (1981), Ecker *et al.* (1980), Evans and Steuer (1973), Gal (1977), Geoffrion (1968), Lowe (1978), Lowe *et al.* (1984), Philip (1972), Steuer (1986), Vincke (1974), Yu and Zeleny (1975), Zionts and Wallenius (1980).

14. SUBSTITUTION RATE

The concept of substitution rate translates the idea of compensation when losing with respect to one criterion while gaining with respect to another. Assume action a is characterized by evaluations $(g_1(a),...,g_j(a),..., g_r(a),...g_n(a))$.

Definition: the *substitution rate at a*, of criterion j with respect to criterion r (taken as a reference criterion) is amount $w_{jr}(a)$ such that, action b, whose evaluations are

$$\left\{ \begin{array}{l} g_l(a) = g_l(b), \quad \forall\ l \neq j,r, \\[2mm] g_j(b) = g_j(a) - 1, \\[2mm] g_r(b) = g_r(a) + w_{jr}(a), \end{array} \right.$$

is indifferent to a.

It is thus the amount which must be added to the reference criterion in order to compensate a loss of one unit on criterion j. The definition of a unit obviously plays an important part in this concept. Roy suggests defining a unit as a difference equivalent to the magnitude of the preference threshold (cf. Chapter 2, section 9).

Let us assume that the decision-maker's global preferences can be represented by a differentiable function $U(g_1,...,g_n)$ aggregating all the criteria. By letting

$$\left\{ \begin{array}{l} z_a = (g_1(a),...,g_n(a)), \\[2mm] z_b = (g_1(b),...,g_n(b)), \end{array} \right.$$

we obtain, as a first approximation:

$$0 = U(z_b) - U(z_a) = \sum_{l=1}^{n} \left(\frac{\partial U}{\partial g_l} \right)_{z_a} (g_l(b) - g_l(a))$$

$$= - \left(\frac{\partial U}{\partial g_j} \right)_{z_a} + w_{jr}(a) \left(\frac{\partial U}{\partial g_r} \right)_{z_a}$$

and from the latter

$$w_{jr}(a) = \frac{(\partial U/\partial g_j)(z_a)}{(\partial U/\partial g_r)(z_a)}.$$

In particular, when function U is a weighted average of the criteria

$$U(g_1,\ldots,g_n) = \sum_{l=1}^{n} \lambda_l g_l,$$

we get

$$w_{jr}(a) = \frac{\lambda_j}{\lambda_r} = \text{constant};$$

in the weighted average case, the substitution rates are equal to the 'weights' of the criteria up to a multiplicative coefficient.

15. PREFERENTIAL INDEPENDENCE

Definition: let F be the family of criteria, J a subset of F and $\bar{J}$ the complementary subset in F; J is *preferentially independent* in F if, given four actions a,b,c,d such that

$$\begin{cases} g_j(a) = g_j(b), & \forall\ j \in \bar{J}, \\ g_j(c) = g_j(d), & \forall\ j \in \bar{J}, \\ g_j(a) = g_j(c), & \forall\ j \in J, \\ g_j(b) = g_j(d), & \forall\ j \in J, \end{cases}$$

we get

$$a\mathrm{P}b \Leftrightarrow c\mathrm{P}d,$$

where P is the global preference relation taking into account all the criteria.

In other words, J is preferentially independent in F if the preferences between actions which differ only by their evaluations according to the criteria in J do not depend upon the values yielded by the criteria of $\bar{J}$.

Other types of independence can be defined (see Keeney and Raiffa, 1976b, for example).

Example

Going back to the example given in section 11, let us assume we have the four following television sets:

	− Price	Picture quality	Sound quality	Maintenance contract
a	− 1500	V.G.	V.G.	G.
b	− 1200	G.	V.G.	G.
c	− 1500	V.G.	A.	N.G.
d	− 1200	G.	A.	N.G.

In order for subset $J = \{$price, picture quality$\}$ to be preferentially independent in F, the preference of *a* over *b* must imply that of *c* over *d*. In other words, the decision-maker prefers to pay 1500 and get a very good picture rather than paying 1200 and getting a good picture, whatever the sound quality and the maintenance contract.

CHAPTER 4

Multiple attribute utility theory

Many didactic and research books have been devoted to multiple attribute utility theory. We will only introduce the subject here; any extra information can be found in two excellent books by Fishburn (1970a) and Keeney and Raiffa (1976b).

1. INTRODUCTION

Multiple attribute utility theory (MAUT) is essentially Anglo-Saxon and is widely used in the United States in decision-aid problems as well as in economic, financial and actuarial problems. The theory is based on the following fundamental axiom: any decision-maker attempts unconsciously (or implicitly) to maximize some function

$$U = U(g_1, g_2, \ldots, g_n),$$

aggregating all the different points of view which are taken into account. In other words, if the decision-maker is asked about his preferences, his answers will be coherent with a certain unknown function U. The role of the researcher is to try to estimate that function by asking the decision-maker some well-chosen questions.

Essentially two types of problems are studied in the frame of this theory:

(1) what properties must the decision-maker's preferences fulfil in order to be able to represent them by a function U with a given analytical form (additive, multiplicative, mixed, etc.);
(2) how can such functions be built and how can the parameters pertaining to the chosen analytical form be estimated?

It is also important to insist on the two following aspects:

(1) Multiple attribute utility theory was developed mostly in the uncertainty case (cf. Chapter 2, section 14) and abundantly calls for probabilities to represent some lack of precision and uncertainty which can appear in a decision problem: the latter aspect deserves more attention as there is no guarantee that the notion of probability is the most suitable in all cases.

(2) Utility theory concerns functions g_j which are true criteria; up to now, only very little research has considered generalizations to other types of criteria (see Roy and Bouyssou, 1987d).

In this chapter, we will only consider the certain case where functions g_j are true criteria.

2. THE ADDITIVE MODEL

The most simple (and most commonly used) analytical form is, of course, the additive form

$$U(a) = \sum_{j=1}^{n} U_j(g_j(a)),$$

where the U_j's are strictly increasing real functions (their only purpose is to transform the criteria in order for them to follow the same scale: this avoids problems of units and ensures that summation makes sense).

Besides the fact that the preferences according to each criterion and the global preference relation must be complete preorder structures (cf. Chapter 2), the additive model imposes the constraint that any subset of criteria be preferentially independent in F (cf. Chapter 3, section 15). Indeed, let J be a subset of criteria and $\bar{J}$ the complementary subset in F, and let a,b,c,d be four actions such that

$$\begin{cases} g_j(a) = g_j(b), & \forall\, j \in \bar{J} \\[2mm] g_j(c) = g_j(d), & \forall\, j \in \bar{J}, \\[2mm] g_j(a) = g_j(c), & \forall\, j \in J, \\[2mm] g_j(b) = g_j(d), & \forall\, j \in J, \end{cases}$$

then we get

$$U(a) - U(b) = \sum_{j \in J} [\, U_j(g_j(a)) - U_j(g_j(b)) \,]$$

$$= \sum_{j \in J} [\, U(g_j(c)) - U(g_j(d)) \,]$$

$$= U(c) - U(d),$$

and therefore,

$$a \mathrm{P} b \Leftrightarrow U(a) - U(b) > 0$$

$$\Leftrightarrow U(c) - U(d) > 0$$

$$\Leftrightarrow c \mathrm{P} d.$$

When A is 'continuously infinite' and $n \geq 3$, this preferential independence is sufficient to ensure an additive form. When A is finite or countable, the necessary and sufficient condition to ensure an additive form is well known theoretically, but impossible to use practically because it involves an infinite number of conditions. The case $n = 2$ has been studied independently quite thoroughly. Note that preferential independence tests can be simplified if one remembers results of the following type: under certain hypotheses, if J and J' are two subsets of criteria which are preferentially independent in F and such that $J \cap J' \neq \varnothing$, $J \setminus J' \neq \varnothing$, $J' \setminus J \neq \varnothing$ and $J \cup J' \neq F$, then $J \cup J'$, $J \cap J'$, $J \setminus J'$, $J' \setminus J$ and $J \vartriangle J'$ are also preferentially independent in F. In such a case, it is sufficient to test the preferential independence of $(n - 1)$ carefully chosen pairs of criteria to be able to deduce preferential independence for any subset of criteria.

In order for differences $U(a) - U(b)$ to have some kind of interpretation in terms of preferences, it is necessary to introduce the concept of independence regarding differences of preferences; for the uncertainty case, the concept of utility independence is introduced.

Concerning all the latter results, extra information can be found in Fishburn (1970a), Krantz *et al.* (1971), Keeney and Raiffa (1976b), Roberts (1979), Suppes *et al.* (1989), Luce *et al.* (1990) and the many papers concerning the subject.

Numerical example

Consider the following valuation table:

	a_1	a_2	a_3	a_4	a_5	a_6	a_7	a_8	a_9
g_1	1	1	1	2	2	2	3	3	3
g_2	1	3	5	1	3	5	1	3	5

and assume that

$$a_9 P a_6 P a_8 P a_5 P a_3 I a_7 P a_2 I a_4 P a_1.$$

The reader can check, as an exercise, that each criterion is preferentially independent in $F=\{g_1,g_2\}$. However, it is not possible to represent the global preference relation by an additive function because

$$a_2 I a_4 \Rightarrow U_1(1) + U_2(3) = U_1(2) + U_2(1),$$

$$a_3 I a_7 \Rightarrow U_1(1) + U_2(5) = U_1(3) + U_2(1),$$

hence, by subtraction,

$$U_2(3) - U_2(5) = U_1(2) - U_1(3),$$

that is

$$U_1(3) + U_2(3) = U_1(2) + U_2(5),$$

contradicting $a_6 P a_8$.

The mayor's problem (cf. Chapter 2, section 18)

The table given here shows the percentages of answers to the first question of the mayor's problem, which are compatible with an additive model for pairs of relations (P,I), $(\rangle,I)$, $(\rangle, \sim)$.

(P,I)	$(\rangle,I)$	$(\rangle, \sim)$
5.39	15.10	15.82

3. OTHER MODELS

Let us first note that, formally, the additive model can be made into a multiplicative one; indeed, by letting

$$U'(a) = e^{U(a)}$$

$$U'_j(g_j(a)) = e^{U_j g_j(a))},$$

we get

$$U'(a) = \prod_{j=1}^{n} U'_j(g_j(a)).$$

The converse is true; this can be proven by using logarithms, under the condition that the functions involved are positive.

It sometimes happens that other models suit the problem at hand better when, for example, preferential independence cannot be verified. From a practical point of view, however, it must be noted that very complex models are of no interest whatsoever. Krantz *et al.* (1971) give some examples of models that are relatively simple (but which cannot be transformed into additive ones) and the conditions that must be verified to be able to use them. For example, a model such that

$$U(a) = [U_1(g_1(a)) + U_2(g_2(a))] \cdot U_3(g_3(a))$$

(or its generalization to more than three criteria) is a simple way to take into account any dependence between criteria.

4. DIRECT METHODS FOR BUILDING THE ADDITIVE MODEL

Direct methods for building the function U consist in estimating functions U_j. A panorama of 24 methods can be found in Fishburn (1967); they are classified according to different aspects: the use or not of probabilities, the type of questions put to the decision-maker, individual building of the U_j's or compensations between them, applicability to the direct or continuous case, and so on. The paper by Farquhar (1984) provides an excellent synthesis of the uncertainty case.

Next, we very briefly describe some examples of such methods. Remember a criterion g_j is a function defined in A which takes its values in a totally ordered set. Let X_j denote this set: its elements will be called possible states of criterion g_j. The table given here shows some examples of what X_j may be.

Point of view j	X_j
Price	[30$, 50$]
Comfort	{bad, average, good, very good}
Ability to achieve something	{yes, no}
Ranking by an expert	{1,2,3,...}

The additive model is thus written

$$U(a) = \sum_{j=1}^{n} U_j(x_j^a),$$

where

$$x_j^a = g_j(a).$$

From now on, x_j and y_j will respectively denote the worst and the best states of X_j.

4.1 FIRST METHOD

Ask the decision-maker to determine the state z_j he considers to be 'the midpoint' of x_j and y_j, then states v_j, midpoint of x_j and z_j, and w_j, midpoint of z_j and y_j, and so on. From this dialogue, which can obviously only be applied when X_j is infinite, we get

$$\begin{cases} U(z_j) = \frac{1}{2}\left[U(x_j) + U(y_j)\right], \\ U(v_j) = \frac{1}{2}\left[U(x_j) + U(z_j)\right], \\ U(w_j) = \frac{1}{2}\left[U(z_j) + U(y_j)\right] \\ \cdots \end{cases}$$

4.2 SECOND METHOD

The decision-maker is asked to determine state z_j such that he considers it equivalent to:

(1) obtain z_j,
(2) obtain x_j with probability ½ and y_j with probability ½.

From there, we get

$$U(z_j) = \tfrac{1}{2}\,[\,U_j(x_j) + U_j(y_j)\,];$$

one then continues with (x_j,z_j), with (z_j,y_j),... This method also assumes that X_j is infinite.

4.3 THIRD METHOD

The decision maker is asked to determine state $z_j(p)$ such that he considers it equivalent to:

(1) obtain $z_j(p)$,
(2) obtain x_j with probability p and y_j with probability $1-p$,

the latter for different values of p. From there, we get

$$U_j(z_j(p)) = p\,U_j(x_j) + (1-p)\,U_j(y_j), \qquad \forall\, p.$$

This method also assumes that X_j is infinite.

4.4 FOURTH METHOD

For each state z_j (or for some of them if there are many), the decision-maker is asked to estimate probability $p(z_j)$ such that he considers it equivalent to:

(1) obtain z_j,
(2) obtain x_j with probability $p(z_j)$ and y_j with probability $1-p(z_j)$.

From there, we get

$$U(z_j) = p(z_j)\,U_j(x_j) + [\,1-p(z_j)\,]\,U_j(y_j).$$

This method can be applied to any set X_j, finite or not.

4.5 FIFTH METHOD

The decision-maker is asked to rank the elements of X_j and to rank the intervals between those elements. The states are then assigned numerical values which respect these rankings (intervals are represented by differences of values). This method is obviously only applicable when X_j is finite.

4.6 SIXTH METHOD

This method assumes that function U_i was built on the basis of i's point of view (by using one of the previous methods, for example): the estimation of U_j is based upon the latter function and the additivity hypothesis.

Let w_i be an arbitrary state in X_i. For each state z_j (or for some of them if there are many), the decision-maker is asked to determine a state t_i in X_i such that he considers it equivalent to:

(1) obtain x_j for j's point of view and w_i for i's point of view,
(2) obtain z_j for j's point of view and t_i and i's point of view.

From there, we get

$$U_j(z_j) = U_j(x_j) + U_i(w_i) - U_i(t_i).$$

This method is applicable to any set X_j, finite or not, but assumes that X_i is infinite.

4.7 SEVENTH METHOD

It can be easily shown that the functions involved can always be transformed in order for the additive model to be written as

$$U(a) = \sum_{j=1}^{n} k_j U_j(x_j^a),$$

where, $\forall j$:

$$\begin{cases} x_j^a = g_j(a), \\ \sum_{j=1}^{n} k_j = 1, \\ U_j(x_j) = 0, \\ U_j(y_j) = 1. \end{cases}$$

Let us then choose two state vectors $(w_i)_{i \neq j}$ and $(t_i)_{i \neq j}$ such that, for any state u_j of X_j, the decision-maker prefers $(u_j,(t_i)_{i \neq j})$ to $(u_j,(w_i)_{i \neq j})$ (this is always possible by preferential independence). The decision-maker is asked to determine state z_j such that he is indifferent between (x_j,t_i) and (z_j,w_i) and also between (z_j,t_i) and (y_j,w_i): from there, we get:

$$\begin{cases} 0 + \sum_{i \neq j} k_i U_i(t_i) = k_j U_j(z_j) + \sum_{i \neq j} k_i U_i(w_i), \\[2em] k_j U_j(z_j) + \sum_{i \neq j} k_i U_i(t_i) = k_j + \sum_{i \neq j} k_i U_i(w_i), \end{cases}$$

hence, by subtraction,

$$U_j(z_j) = \tfrac{1}{2}.$$

By asking similar questions, one can determine the states of respective values $\tfrac{1}{4}$, $\tfrac{3}{4}$, $\tfrac{1}{8}$, $\tfrac{3}{8}$,... (this method is obviously only applicable when X_j is infinite).

In order to estimate the values of the k_j's, one must try to obtain $(n-1)$ pairs of indifferent actions: the $(n-1)$ corresponding linear equations, together with the fact that the sum of the k_j's is 1, allows their value to be determined.

The questions which are put to the decision-maker in this method imply comparisons between n-dimensional state vectors, i.e. real or fictive actions. There is not, as there was previously, any introduction of preference intensities, probabilities, or pairwise comparisons between states. In that way, the method only uses concepts from the basic axiomatics of additive models; it must be noted, however, that the questions are quite sophisticated and are all the more complicated because they often involve fictive actions.

5. AN INDIRECT METHOD FOR BUILDING THE ADDITIVE MODEL: UTA

Indirect methods for building the function U consist in estimating it on the basis of the global judgements made by the decision-maker on set A. In fact, they generalize methods such as discriminant analysis or multiple regression which concern the case where

$$U(a) = \sum_{j=1}^{n} k_j g_j(a).$$

As an example, we present here under the UTA (Utilité Additive) method, due to Jacquet-Lagrèze and Siskos (1982b).

THE UTA METHOD

This method consists in first determining an 'optimal' utility function through linear programming and then performing a sensitivity analysis. It assumes the criteria are expressed in numerical form, i.e. that the elements of X_j (which can be finite or infinite) are real numbers. As previously, we denote by x_j and y_j respectively the best and worst states of X_j, i.e. the smallest and largest number in X_j. Interval $[x_j, y_j]$ is divided into r_j 'equidistant' intervals, denoted by $[u_j^l, u_j^{l+1}]$, $l = 1, \ldots, r_j$, where

$$u_j^l = x_j + \frac{l-1}{r_j}(y_j - x_j).$$

The method consists in determining the $U_j(u_j^l)$'s and executing linear interpolations between those points.

Thus, if $z_j \in [u_j^l, u_j^{l+1}]$, we get

$$U_j(z_j) = U_j(u_j^l) + \frac{z_j - u_j^l}{u_j^{l+1} - u_j^l}[U_j(u_j^{l+1}) - U_j(u_j^l)].$$

When the number of elements of X_j is small, those elements are taken as values for the u_j^l's.

Let

$$U(a) = \sum_{j=1}^{n} U_j(x_j^a) + \sigma(a),$$

where

$$x_j^a = g_j(a),$$

and $\sigma(a)$ is the error associated with the estimation of $U(a)$. Assuming a subset A' of actions is at hand for which the decision-maker's preferences are known and constitute a complete preorder, the constraints to be satisfied are the following: $\forall\ a, b \in A'$:

$$
\left\{
\begin{array}{l}
U(a) - U(b) > 0 \text{ if } aPb, \\[2ex]
U(a) - U(b) = 0 \text{ if } aIb, \\[2ex]
U_j(u_j^{l+1}) - U_j(u_j^l) > 0, \ \forall \ j, \ \forall \ l, \\[2ex]
\sum_{j=1}^{n} U_j(y_j) = 1 \text{ (normalization)} \\[2ex]
U_j(x_j) = 0, \ \forall \ j, \\[2ex]
U_j(u_j^l) \geq 0, \ \sigma(a) \geq 0,
\end{array}
\right.
$$

where $U(a)$ and $U(b)$ are replaced by their expressions in functions of variables u_j^l, $\sigma(a)$ and $\sigma(b)$.

The first step of the method consists in determining those variables in a way which minimizes

$$
\sum_{a \in A'} \sigma(a).
$$

One must thus solve a linear program involving

$$
Q + 2 \sum_{q=1}^{Q} (n_q - 1) + \sum_{j=1}^{n} r_j
$$

constraints (transitivity of P and I allows to eliminate many redundant constraints) and

$$
\sum_{j=1}^{n} r_j + \sum_{q=1}^{Q} n_q
$$

variables, where Q is the number of indifference classes of the complete preorder on A' and where n_q ($q = 1, 2, \ldots, Q$) is the number of actions in the qth class. The strict positivity constraints are replaced by inequalities in which the right-hand sides are small positive numbers (which can, in fact, be interpreted as indifference thresholds).

This first step thus yields a function U which is the sum of partial piecewise linear utility functions. This function is rather arbitrary since it depends upon the choice of the criterion which has been minimized, that is the sum of errors $\sigma(a)$. Indeed, if the latter minimum is zero, the polyhedron defined by the constraints is nonempty and there are thus many functions U which can represent the decision-maker's preferences exactly on set A'. If the minimum is not zero, those preferences cannot be represented exactly by a function U; the function which represents preferences 'the best' then depends upon the chosen criterion: for example, the complete preorder corresponding to the function which is the optimal solution of the above-mentioned linear program is not necessarily the closest (in the sense of the classical Kendall or Spearman indices) to the complete preorder given by the decision-maker. This is why the authors of the UTA method proposed a second step during which the neighbourhood of the obtained solution is explored. The latter exploration is achieved by adding the following inequality to the system of constraints of the previous step

$$\sum_{a \in A'} \sigma(a) \leq F^* + \Delta,$$

where F^* is the minimal value obtained from the previous step and Δ is a very small percentage of F^*. By minimizing and maximizing, under this new system of constraints, functions

$$\sum_{j=1}^{n} \rho_j U_j(y_j)$$

where $\rho_j = 0$ or 1, $\forall\, j$, and this for several different series of values of the ρ_j's, a sample of solutions is generated, that is a set of utility functions which are suitable for the representation of the decision-maker's preferences.

From the latter information, one can derive either a unique function, such as in PREFCALC (next section), or a deterministic or fuzzy 'outranking relation' (see, for example, Jacquet-Lagrèze, 1981). All references for the many real-life applications of this method, along with some possible extensions can be found in Jacquet-Lagrèze and Siskos (1982b).

6. A DECISION-AID SOFTWARE BASED UPON THE ADDITIVE MODEL: PREFCALC
(Jacquet-Lagrèze, 1984a, 1990)

The data needed by the software are the following:

(1) a set of actions and their evaluations, under numerical form, according to a set of criteria;

(2) for each criterion, the extreme values x_j and y_j which are suitable for the decision-maker and number r_j of linear pieces which will make up function U_j associated with this criterion (in order to use the UTA method described in the previous section).

The flowchart given below summarizes the operations which may be performed in a decision-aiding process. As one can easily see, the method consists in building an (additive) utility function on the basis of a set of reference actions and then applying it to the set of all actions. Building the utility function based upon the reference set can be achieved indirectly (option 1) or directly (option 2).

6.1 OPTION 1

The decision-maker is asked to rank the actions in the reference set and, using the UTA method (previous section), a utility function is built and is then proposed to the decision-maker. More precisely:

Flow chart

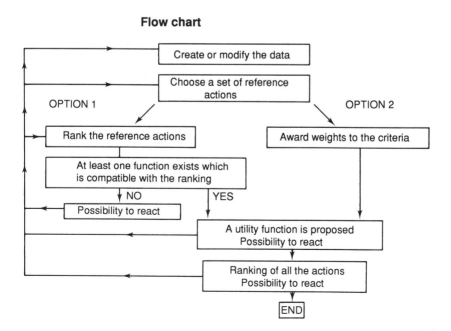

(1) If the minimum obtained by solving the linear program of step 1 of the UTA method is strictly positive (which means that no additive utility function can represent exactly the preferences given by the decision-maker on the reference set), then the utility function proposed is the one which yields that minimum and the second step of the UTA method is not necessary. However, the decision-maker must be made aware of the fact that no function is entirely compatible with his ranking; in particular, any preference contradicting the dominance relation is explicitly mentioned and the decision-maker can revise his ranking on the reference set at any time.

(2) If the minimum is zero (which means that there is one and thus an infinite number of functions which are compatible with the given preferences), then the second step of the UTA method is applied and, on the basis of the sample of generated solutions, an 'average' utility function is proposed to the decision-maker.

6.2 OPTION 2

In the frame of a model of the following type

$$U(a) = \sum_{j=1}^{n} U_j(g_j(a)),$$

where

$$\sum_{j=1}^{n} U_j(y_j) = 1,$$

the values $U_j(y_j)$ can be considered as representatives of the relative importance awarded to the criteria since their sum is 1: moreover, if $U_k(y_k) = 1$ for some criterion k, all other functions U_j ($j \neq k$) are zero and $U(a) = U_k(g_k(a))$, i.e. only criterion k is taken into account. Option 2 consists in asking the decision-maker to assign 'weights' to the criteria by associating a number p_j (between 0 and 9) to each criterion j in the increasing order of importance he gives to the criteria. From there,

$$U_j(y_j) = \frac{p_j}{\sum_{h=1}^{n} p_h}.$$

In order to be able to rapidly propose to the decision-maker a utility function to which he can react, the method does not require, at this stage, any extra information on functions U_j, but directly proposes the following functions (remember x_j, y_j and r_j were specified in the initial data):

$$\begin{cases} U_j(u_j^l) = \sqrt{\dfrac{u_j^l - x_j}{y_j - x_j}} \cdot U_j(y_j), & l = 1,\dots,r_j + 1 \\[2mm] U_j \text{ linear between the values } u_j^l, \end{cases}$$

where the u_j^l's are the first coordinates of the linear pieces making up U_j (cf. first step of the UTA method).

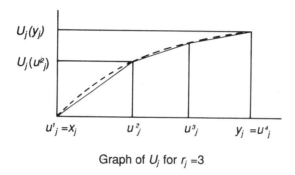

Graph of U_j for $r_j = 3$

The latter formula is obviously completely arbitrary but it gives function U_j a concave shape which corresponds to an attitude often encountered. Furthermore, that choice is not very important since the decision-maker can subsequently modify function U_j.

The utility function, determined by option 1 or option 2, is then proposed to the decision-maker under the form of a set of graphs representing functions U_j. The resulting ranking on the reference set is also presented. At this stage, the decision-maker can go back and modify some data (acceptable extreme values for the criteria, number of linear pieces), change the ranking on the reference set or correct some of the weights.

When the utility function is accepted, it is applied to the set of all actions in order to rank them. The decision-maker can then end the procedure or go back to a previous step.

PREFCALC was one of the first software packages on the market designed to be easy to use. The collection of data (which can be achieved through a word processor or some software like dBASE II), the presentation of many graphics, the possibility given, at any moment, to go back, modify data, and observe the effects of the modifications, make it an efficient tool for decision-aid. We could have left the presentation of this software to the chapter on interactive methods: we chose to put it here on the one hand because the procedure is based upon the estimation of an additive utility function and, on the other hand, because the interaction with the decision-maker is directed more toward the construction of a model of his preferences than toward the set of actions itself, this last option being one of the characteristics of what we call an interactive method.

7. THE ANALYTIC HIERARCHY PROCESS
(Saaty, 1980)

It is impossible, in the frame of this book, to give a detailed description of this methodology and of the large amount of comments it gave rise to (see, for example, Belton, 1986). Briefly, it encompasses the following three steps:

(1) The decision problem is represented as a hierarchy in which the top vertex is the main objective of the problem, the bottom vertices are the actions and the intermediary vertices represent the criteria (which are more and more aggregated as one goes higher in the hierarchy) which should be taken into account.
(2) At each level of the hierarchy, a pairwise comparison of the vertices is performed from the point of view of their 'contribution' to each of the higher-level vertices to which they are linked. The pairwise comparison is made in terms of 'preference ratios' (if they are actions) or 'importance ratios' (if they are criteria) evaluated on a numerical scale proposed within the method; the information thereby obtained is generally redundant (if the number of pairwise comparisons is high) and more or less incoherent (the ratio between a and c isn't always exactly equal to the product of the ratio between a and b by that between b and c). However, a mathematical technique based upon the computation of the eigenvalues of the matrix of pairwise comparisons, allows the calculation of the value to be given to each element in order for the matrix of their pairwise ratios be the closest (in terms of some distance) to the matrix of pairwise comparisons given by the decision-maker.

(3) When each vertex of the hierarchy has been evaluated from the point of view of its contribution to the vertices of the immediately higher level, the global contribution of each action to the main objective is calculated by an aggregation of the weighted average type.

This method led to the development of a software package (EXPERT CHOICE) and seems to be constantly applied to real-life problems.

Chapter 5

Outranking methods

1. INTRODUCTION

As was shown in the previous chapter, methods based upon multiple attribute utility theory lead to a function allowing the ranking of all actions from best to worst. The result thereby obtained is thus quite rich with respect to the dominance relation, which is the only 'objective' element one can extract from the data in a multicriteria problem. In fact, the large amount of information contained in the result is due to the theory's strong assumptions (existence of function U, additivity, etc.) and to all the extra information demanded from the decision-maker (preference intensities, substitution rates). One may wonder whether it is always necessary to go that far in the frame of decision aid. Considering a choice problem, for example: if it is known that some action a is better than b and c, it becomes irrelevant to analyse preferences between b and c. Those two actions can perfectly remain incomparable without endangering the decision-aid procedure. Also, solving a decision problem is a temporal process during the course of which preferences evolve as new information becomes available. It is thus quite important to have concepts at hand with which we are able to model the situation during the decision procedure, i.e. when some actions are still incomparable. Finally, a conclusion of incomparability between some actions may also be quite helpful since it puts forward some aspects of the problem which would perhaps deserve a more thorough study. By limiting the objective of a method to building a complete preorder (as in multiple attribute utility theory, or, more trivially, by using a weighted sum of the criteria), one runs the risk of ending with a complete preorder even when the data do not justify it.

All those considerations led to the development of outranking methods. The underlying idea is thus that it is better to accept a result less rich than the one yielded by multiple attribute utility theory, if one can avoid introducing mathematical hypotheses which are too strong and asking the decision-maker questions which are too intricate. The result is thus, in general, in between the dominance relation (too poor to be useful) and the multiple attribute utility function (too rich to really be reliable). In other words, what is attempted in these methods is to enrich the dominance relation by some elements which suffer no discussion, by strongly established preferences.

The concept of outranking is due to B. Roy, who can be considered as the founder of these methods.

Definition (Roy, 1974): an *outranking relation* is a binary relation S defined in A such that aSb if, given what is known about the decision-maker's preferences and given the quality of the valuations of the actions and the nature of the problem, there are enough arguments to decide that a is at least as good as b, while there is no essential reason to refute that statement.

Obviously, the latter is not a precise mathematical definition but rather a general idea. The outranking methods which have been proposed in the literature differ, among other aspects, by the way they formalize that definition.

There is obviously no reason for an outranking relation to be complete or transitive. It does not allow one, in general, to immediately obtain a better compromise or a ranking of the actions. An outranking method can thus be divided into two steps: building the outranking relation (cf. Roy, 1989) and exploiting it with regard to the chosen statement of the problem (cf. Vanderpooten, 1990b).

Most outranking methods were proposed for problems in which the set A of actions is finite but the general philosophy of such methods is obviously applicable to infinite cases.

Important remark: most of the following methods involve a notion of 'weights' of the criteria, for the representation of their relative importance. We will not go into procedures to determine those weights in this chapter, but we will come back to that problem in Chapter 7.

2. THE ELECTRE I METHOD (Roy, 1968)

This method was built for multicriteria choice problems: its aim is therefore to be able to obtain a subset N of actions such that any action which is not in N is outranked by at least one action of N. The latter subset (which will be made as small as possible) is thus not the set of good actions, but it is the set in which the best compromise can certainly be found.

2.1 BUILDING OF THE OUTRANKING RELATION

Each criterion is assigned a weight p_j, increasing with the importance of the criterion, and to each ordered pair (a,b) of actions is associated the following concordance index:

$$c(a,b) = \frac{1}{P} \sum_{j:g_j(a) \geq g_j(b)} p_j, \qquad \text{where } P = \sum_{j=1}^{n} p_j.$$

The latter index, taking its values between 0 and 1, can be seen as measuring the arguments in favour of the statement 'a outranks b'. Among the criteria in favour of b, some may shed some doubt upon the latter statement. In the initial version of ELECTRE I, this phenomenon was represented by a discordance index defined as follows:

$$d(a,b) = \begin{cases} 0 \text{ if } g_j(a) \geq g_j(b), \forall j, \\ \\ \frac{1}{\delta} \max_j [g_j(b) - g_j(a)], \text{ otherwise,} \end{cases}$$

where

$$\delta = \max_{c,d,j} [g_j(c) - g_j(d)].$$

$d(a,b)$ is thus an index (taking its values between 0 and 1) which increases if the preference of b over a becomes very large for at least one criterion. However, one can easily see that this index can only be used if differences $g_j(b) - g_j(a)$ make some sense (thereby excluding qualitative criteria) and are comparable from one criterion to another. If those assumptions are not verified, it is preferable to define, for each criterion j, a discordance set D_j made of ordered pairs (x_j, y_j) such that if

$$g_j(a) = x_j \text{ and } g_j(b) = y_j,$$

then the outranking of b by a is refused (see the numerical example given below).

Having then defined a (relatively large) concordance threshold $\hat{c}$, and, if necessary, a (relatively small) discordance threshold $\hat{d}$, an outranking relation S is defined by:

$$aSb \text{ iff} \begin{cases} c(a,b) \geq \hat{c}, \\ \\ d(a,b) \leq \hat{d}, \end{cases}$$

or

$$aSb \text{ iff} \begin{cases} c(a,b) \geq \hat{c}, \\ \\ (g_j(a), g_j(b)) \notin D_j, \forall j, \end{cases}$$

according to the way in which discordance was defined.

2.2 EXPLOITATION OF THE OUTRANKING RELATION

Having outranking S, which can be represented by a graph in which vertices represent actions, one seeks a subset N of actions such that:

$$\begin{cases} \forall b \in A \setminus N, \ \exists a \in N: aSb, \\ \\ \forall a,b \in N, \ a\cancel{S}b. \end{cases}$$

One aims to find a subset N of actions such that any action which is not in N is outranked by at least one action of N and the actions of N are incomparable (the latter condition allows to render N minimal for inclusion). In graph theory, this type of set is called a kernel of the graph and there exist procedures to determine it. Let us also recall that if the graph has no circuit, the kernel exists and is unique. One possible technique thus consists in reducing the initial graph's circuits (i.e. replacing each circuit by a unique element, which is equivalent to considering the actions in the circuit as tied), but the latter operation may eliminate a great deal of the information contained in the outranking relation. Another technique consists in using the concept of minimum weakness quasi-kernel (see Hansen *et al.*, 1976; Vincke, 1977).

In order to advance towards the best possible compromise, a more refined analysis of the kernel's actions must be performed. Practically, it is advised to use fluctuations of the method's parameters $(p_j, \hat{c}, \hat{d})$ and to study the robustness of the result with respect to those variations. The latter robustness analysis can also be used to break up ties between the kernel's actions.

2.3 NUMERICAL EXAMPLE

Suppose a consumer wishes to buy a new car. Seven types of cars are proposed. The criteria taken into consideration are the price, comfort, speed and design. The table below contains the relevant data along with the weights assigned to the different criteria.

	1	2	3	4	5	6	7	Weight
Price	300	250	250	200	200	200	100	5
Comfort	E	E	A	A	A	W	W	4
Speed	F	A	F	F	A	F	A	3
Design	S	S	S	O	S	S	O	3

(E = excellent; A = average; W = weak; F = fast; S = superior; O = ordinary)

Concordance indexes are given in the next table (they should be multiplied by $\frac{1}{15}$).

	1	2	3	4	5	6	7
1	—	10	10	10	10	10	10
2	12	—	12	7	10	7	10
3	11	11	—	10	10	10	10
4	8	8	12	—	12	12	10
5	8	11	12	12	—	12	10
6	11	11	11	11	11	—	10
7	5	8	5	8	8	9	—

Discordance is defined as follows: the outranking of b by a is refused in the three following cases:

	Price	Price	Comfort
a	300	250	W
b	100	100	E

For $p = \dfrac{12}{15}$, one obtains an outranking relation which is represented by its graph.

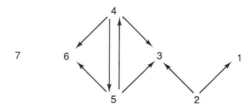

The graph's kernels are subsets {2,4,7} and {2,5,7}, 4 and 5 considered as being tied.

2.4 THE SOFTWARE ELECTRE IS (Roy and Skalka, 1984a)

Anyone interested will find in the reference given above, a user's manual of software inspired by ELECTRE I, including an adaptation to the case where the criteria are pseudo-criteria. The main objective of this software is the determination of the kernel of the outranking relation, after eventual reduction of circuits.

2.5 COMMENTS

The ELECTRE I method must be given credit for being the first outranking method to appear in the literature: it was the starting point for a great deal of methodological work and real-life applications. Even if subsequent methods take into account much more the great progress made in the field of preference modelling, ELECTRE I remains the typical example of the outranking approach.

3. THE ELECTRE II METHOD
   (Roy and Bertier, 1971b, 1973)

As seen above, the ELECTRE I method is designed for choice problems, by the way in which the outranking relation is exploited. The ELECTRE II method, on the other hand, aims to rank the actions from best to worst (ranking problem).

3.1 BUILDING OF THE OUTRANKING RELATION

One could obviously use the same building technique as in the previous method. However, the authors introduced some variations which we recall here.

Concordance and discordance having been defined as in the ELECTRE I method, two concordance thresholds $\hat{c}_1$ and $\hat{c}_2$ such that $\hat{c}_1 > \hat{c}_2$, a strong outranking relation S^F and a weak outranking relation S^f are built as follows:

$$a S^F b \text{ iff} \begin{cases} c(a,b) \geq \hat{c}_1, \\ \sum_{j:g_j(a)>g_j(b)} p_j > \sum_{j:g_j(a)<g_j(b)} p_j, \\ (g_j(a),g_j(b)) \notin D_j, \ \forall \ j; \end{cases}$$

$$a S^f b \text{ iff} \begin{cases} c(a,b) \geq \hat{c}_2, \\ \sum_{j:g_j(a)>g_j(b)} p_j > \sum_{j:g_j(a)<g_j(b)} p_j, \\ (g_j(a),g_j(b)) \notin D_j, \ \forall \ j. \end{cases}$$

Discordance may also give rise to two severity levels by building, for each criterion j, two discordance sets D_j^1 and D_j^2 such that $D_j^2 \subset D_j^1$.

3.2 EXPLOITATION OF THE OUTRANKING RELATION

The class of best actions (the first class of the ranking) is obtained as follows: after reducing the circuits of S^F (cf. ELECTRE I), one determines set B of actions which are not strongly outranked by any other action; inside that set, the circuits of S^f are reduced and one determines the set A^1 of actions which are not weakly outranked by any other action of B. Set A^1 is the first class of the ranking and the procedure is started again in the remaining set, thereby yielding a complete preorder.

A second complete preorder is built in an analogous way but by starting with the class of worst actions (those which outrank no other action) and 'going up' toward the best actions.

The two preorders obtained are, in general, not the same: if they are close, the decision-maker is offered a 'median preorder' (for details, see Roy and Bertier, 1971b). Otherwise, a more thorough study is required since it is possible that the data are too divergent to be able to build an acceptable complete preorder. In both cases, a robustness analysis is obviously necessary.

Note, for example, that if a certain action doesn't outrank any other and is itself outranked by no other (in other words, if it is difficult to compare it with the others), it will appear as first in the first ranking and as last in the second: the comparison between the two complete preorders is thus quite useful to detect 'problematic' actions. This is why it is advised to build the partial preorder resulting from the insersection of the two complete preorders (cf. Chapter 2, section 10.2).

Another way to obtain the complete preorders is based upon the degrees of the graph's vertices, i.e. the number of actions which strongly outrank and which are strongly outranked by each action, ties being eliminated on the basis of the weak outranking relation.

3.3 COMMENTS

The ELECTRE II method is undoubtedly the best known and most widely used outranking method: many examples of real-life applications can be found in the references given in Chapter 7, section 13.

4. THE ELECTRE III METHOD (Roy, 1978)

The ELECTRE I and ELECTRE II methods (at least their initial versions) concern problems involving true criteria. With the development of preference modelling, some new procedures appeared which take explicitly into account indifference and preference thresholds. The ELECTRE III method is a good example of the latter; furthermore, it has the peculiarity of being based upon a valued outranking relation which has the property, with respect to an ordinary relation, of being less sensitive to variations of the data and involved parameters. As in ELECTRE II, we are concerned with a ranking problem.

4.1 BUILDING OF THE VALUED OUTRANKING RELATION

The valued outranking relation of the ELECTRE III method is characterized by the definition of an outranking degree $S(a,b)$ associated with each ordered pair (a,b) of actions, representing the more or less great *outranking credibility* of a over b. The latter degree, taking its values between 0 and 1, is so large that the outranking of b by a is 'strong'; it is thus an increasing function of $g_j(a)$, $\forall j$ and a decreasing function of $g_j(b)$, $\forall j$.

A weight p_j having been associated with each pseudo-criterion g_j, the following concordance index is computed for each ordered pair (a,b) of actions:

$$c(a,b) = \frac{1}{P} \sum_{j=1}^{n} p_j c_j(a,b), \qquad \text{where } P = \sum_{j=1}^{n} p_j$$

and where

$$c_j(a,b) = \begin{cases} 1 \text{ if } g_j(a) + q_j(g_j(a)) \geq g_j(b), \\ 0 \text{ if } g_j(a) + p_j(g_j(a)) \leq g_j(b), \\ \text{linear between the two,} \end{cases}$$

q_j and p_j denoting the indifference and preference thresholds respectively: the definition of $c_j(a,b)$ is illustrated by the figure given here.

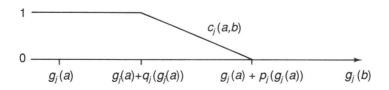

Note that if criteria g_j are quasi-criteria, i.e. if $q_j(g_j(a)) = p_j(g_j(a))$, $\forall$ a and $\forall$ j, then the concordance index becomes

$$c(a,b) = \frac{1}{P} \sum_{j:g_j(a)+q_j(g_j(a)) \geq g_j(b)} p_j = \frac{1}{P} \sum_{\substack{j:aP_jb \\ \text{or } aI_jb}} p_j,$$

where (P_j, I_j) is the semiorder structure associated with criterion j.

The latter index is identical to the one used in the ELECTRE I and II methods if criteria g_j are true criteria (thresholds equal to zero).

The definition of discordance requires the introduction of a veto threshold $v_j(g_j(a))$ (function of $g_j(a)$) for each criterion j such that any credibility for the outranking of b by a is refused if

$$g_j(b) \geq g_j(a) + v_j(g_j(a)),$$

the latter even if all the other criteria are in favour of the outranking of b by a.

A discordance index, for each criterion, is then defined by

$$D_j(a,b) = \begin{cases} 0 \text{ if } g_j(b) \leq g_j(a) + p_j(g_j(a)), \\ 1 \text{ if } g_j(b) \geq g_j(a) + v_j(g_j(a)), \\ \text{linear between two,} \end{cases}$$

as illustrated by the figure.

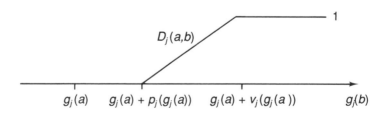

Finally, the degree of outranking is defined by

$$S(a,b) = \begin{cases} c(a,b) \text{ if } D_j(a,b) \leq c(a,b), \ \forall \ j, \\ c(a,b) . \prod_{j \in J(a,b)} \frac{1 - D_j(a,b)}{1 - c(a,b)}, \end{cases}$$

where $J(a,b)$ is the set of criteria for which $D_j(a,b) > c(a,b)$. The degree of outranking is thus equal to the concordance index when no criterion is discordant; in the opposite case, the concordance index is lowered in function of the importance of the discordances.

4.2 EXPLOITATION OF THE VALUED OUTRANKING RELATION

Value $\lambda = \max\limits_{a,b \in A} S(a,b)$ is determined and only the arcs having values 'sufficiently close' to λ are considered, i.e. more precisely, those which have a value larger or equal to $\lambda - s(\lambda)$, where $s(\lambda)$ is a threshold to be determined (it allows the values close enough to λ to be defined). The latter yields a non-valued outranking relation for which the qualification $Q(a)$ of each action a can be computed (that is the number of actions which are outranked by a minus the number of actions which outrank a). The set of actions having the largest qualification will be called the *first distillate D_1*.

If D_1 only contains one action, the previous procedure is started again in $A \smallsetminus D_1$. Otherwise, the same procedure is applied inside D_1; if distillate D_2 which is thereby obtained is a singleton, the procedure is started again in $D_1 \smallsetminus D_2$ (except if the latter set is empty); otherwise, it is applied inside D_2, and so forth until D_1 is used up entirely, before starting with $A \smallsetminus D_1$. This procedure, which is called a descending distillation chain, yields a first complete preorder.

A second complete preorder is obtained by an ascending distillation chain, in which the actions having the smallest qualification are first retained.

The information which can be drawn from these two preorders is analogous to that obtained by ELECTRE II. For an example of robustness analysis, we recommend the work of Roy, Present and Silhol mentioned in Chapter 7, section 13.

4.3 COMMENTS

As can be readily seen, the ELECTRE III method is much more sophisticated than ELECTRE II; it also involves a great number of technical parameters which must be fixed by the analyst, with no possible physical interpretation whatsoever. It must be given credit for involving some aspects which are often neglected in other methods and for yielding relatively stable results, but many researchers consider it to be too complicated and hard to interpret. Finally, some research is currently being done to refine the exploitation of the valued outranking relation which, in some cases, may lead, in its present form, to results contradicting intuition.

5. THE ELECTRE IV METHOD
(Hugonnard and Roy, 1982)

The ELECTRE IV method, as the previous one, is based upon the consideration of a family of pseudo-criteria; it aims to rank the actions, but without introducing any weighting of the criteria.

5.1 BUILDING OF THE OUTRANKING RELATION

Two relations are built (one strong S_F and one weak S_f) on the basis of 'common sense' considerations compatible with the lack of information on the relative importance of the criteria: $\forall j$, let P_j and Q_j respectively denote the strong and weak preferences associated with pseudo-criterion g_j (Chapter 2, section 9), and v_j denote the veto threshold on that criterion (cf. ELECTRE III). We get:

aS_Fb if no criterion exists for which b is strongly preferred to a and if the number of criteria for which b is weakly preferred to a is at most equal to the number of criteria for which a is preferred (weakly or strongly) to b;

aS_fb if no criterion exists for which b is strongly preferred to a but the second condition for the strong outranking is not fulfilled; or if there exists a unique criterion for which b is strictly preferred to a, under the condition that the difference in favour of b is not larger than the veto threshold and that a is strictly preferred to b for at least half of the criteria.

5.2 EXPLOITATION OF THE OUTRANKING RELATION

The exploitation is performed as in ELECTRE III (distillations) but is made simpler by the fact that there are only two outranking levels. One determines the subset D_1 of actions which have the largest qualification in A for S_F (remember that the qualification of a is the number of actions outranked by a, minus the number of actions which outrank a). If D_1 is a singleton, qualifications are computed again in $A \setminus D_1$ and the subset D_2 of actions which have the largest qualification in $A \setminus D_1$ for S_F is determined, and so forth. When a D_h contains more than one action, the same procedure is applied inside D_h but on the basis of relation S_f. This descending procedure is ended when all the actions are ranked in a complete preorder. A second complete preorder is built by an ascending procedure (by determining each time the actions which have the smallest qualification). The information drawn from these two procedures is analogous to that obtained in ELECTRE II or ELECTRE III.

5.3 COMMENTS

The problem of the determination of weights in outranking methods has always been a major preoccupation for researchers (we will come back to this in Chapter 7). The ELECTRE IV method avoids the latter problem by making the assumption that there is no relation of more or less relative importance on the criteria. Note that this does not mean that all the criteria are of the same importance; on the other hand, it does imply that no criterion is negligible with respect to any other. It is obvious that the 'common sense' considerations displayed here to build relations S_F and S_f can be modified in function of the considered application.

6. METHODS INVOLVING AN IMPORTANCE RELATION ON THE CRITERIA

The origin of the previous method lies in the fact that one needed a method which did not require a definition of weights for the criteria, because their relative importance was unknown. Other authors considered the case in which an importance relation on the criteria is at hand, but there is no desire to quantify by weights. Essentially three methods were proposed in that context.

The QUALIFLEX method (Paelinck, 1978; Janssen et al., 1990) consists in exploring the set of weights which are compatible with the importance relation on the criteria (assumed to be a complete preorder) and, for each of them, to determine the ranking of the actions which is at minimum distance from the weighted average of the rankings yielded by the criteria.

The ORESTE method (Roubens, 1981) combines, in a rather mysterious way, the ranks of the actions on the criteria with the ranks of the criteria themselves (the importance relation on the criteria is also a complete preorder), in order to obtain a global rank for each ordered pair (action, criterion) to be used as the basis for comparing actions. The recent work by Pastijn and Leysen (1989) brings some new light on the interpretation of the parameters of the method.

The MELCHIOR method (Leclercq, 1984) is in fact the only one which does not introduce quantitative aspects in the treatment of the data and it contains, as a particular case, the ELECTRE IV method. We describe its main features in the following section.

We must also mention the lexicographic method, which will be considered in Chapter 7, in the section devoted to 'elementary' multicriteria methods.

7. MELCHIOR: A PURELY ORDINAL METHOD
   (Leclercq, 1984)

A family of n pseudo-criteria is at hand, provided with a relation T such that $i\mathrm{T}j$ means: 'criterion i is at least as important as criterion j'. No assumption is made beforehand on the properties of T. The basic idea is to say that a outranks b if the criteria which are unfavourable to the latter assertion are 'hidden' by those which are in its favour and if no criterion j exists such that $g_j(b) > g_j(a) + v_j$, where v_j is a veto threshold (no discordance).

It remains to define what we call:

(1) criteria which are in favour of the outranking of b by a,
(2) criteria which are unfavourable to the outranking of b by a,
(3) 'to hide'.

The author of the method proposes the following definitions:

(1) A criterion j will be said to be in favour of the outranking of b by a if

$$a\mathrm{P}_j b \qquad \text{(1st definition)}$$

or

$$a(\mathrm{P}_j \cup \mathrm{Q}_j)b \qquad \text{(2nd definition)}$$

or

$$g_j(a) > g_j(b) \qquad \text{(3rd definition).}$$

(2) A criterion j will be said to be unfavourable to the outranking of b by a if

$$b\mathrm{P}_j a \qquad \text{(1st definition)}$$

or

$$b(P_j \cup Q_j)a \quad \text{(2nd definition)}$$

or

$$g_j(b) > g_j(a) \quad \text{(3rd definition)}.$$

(3) A subfamily G of criteria 'hides' a subfamily H of criteria if, for any criterion j of H, there exists a criterion i of G such that

$$i\text{T}j \qquad \text{(1st definition)}$$

or

$$i\text{T}j \text{ or not } (j\text{T}i) \quad \text{(2nd definition)},$$

the same criterion i of G not being allowed to hide several criteria of H.

Obviously, other definitions could be introduced.

By choosing two combinations of definitions, one stricter than the other, one obtains a strong and a weak outranking relations which are in turn exploited as in the ELECTRE IV method (the latter in fact coincides with MELCHIOR in the particular case where T is empty). Let us note here that the choice of combinations of definitions is not arbitrary. Leclercq (1984) gives examples of coherent combinations, a study of the properties of the resulting outranking relations and a numerical example.

8. TRICHOTOMIC SEGMENTATION
(Moscarola and Roy, 1977; Roy, 1981a)

The procedure described in this section was built in order to help a decision-maker who must, during the process of discovering the actions, decide to which category he will assign them among several defined in respect of the treatment they will receive later; this kind of situation occurs, for example, in loan allocation problems, when launching new products or research projects, when awarding promotions, and so on. As indicated by its name, this procedure is limited to the case where there are three categories considered: K^+, K^- and $K^?$ (in the example of loan allocation, they correspond to 'accepting', 'refusing' and 'awaiting extra information').

Assume the considered actions are evaluated through criteria $g_1, g_2, \ldots, g_n$. The procedure consists in fixing (with the decision-maker's help) some pairs $\{\bar{b}^k, \bar{c}^k\}$, $k = 1, 2, \ldots, l$ of n-dimensional vectors such that if

$$g_j(a) \geq b_j^k, \ \forall \ j,$$

for at least one value of k, then a is assigned to K^+; if

$$g_j(a) \leq c_j^k, \ \forall \ j,$$

for at least one value of k, then a is assigned to K^-; if

$$b_j^k \geq g_j(a) \geq c_j^k, \ \forall \ j,$$

for at least one value of k, then a is assigned to $K^?$. Intuitively, the $\bar{b}^k$'s correspond to 'high profiles' for which the decision-maker chooses category K^+ without any hesitation (he agrees to award a loan) and the $\bar{c}^k$'s correspond to 'low profiles' for which the decision-maker chooses category K^- without any hesitation (he refuses to award a loan). There is a one-to-one correspondence between the $\bar{b}^k$'s and the $\bar{c}^k$'s so that any action offering a profile between a $\bar{b}^k$ and a $\bar{c}^k$ (for the same value of k) is assigned to category $K^?$.

Of course, many actions are in neither of the three situations described above. The authors therefore recommend to compute, for each action a, the following outranking indexes:

$$S(a, b^k), \ S(b^k, a), \ S(a, c^k), \ S(c^k, a), \qquad k = 1, 2, \ldots, l$$

where b^k and c^k respectively denote fictive actions such that

$$\begin{cases} g_j(b^k) = b_j^k, \ \forall \ j, \\ g_j(c^k) = c_j^k, \ \forall \ j, \end{cases}$$

and where outranking indexes are computed as in the ELECTRE III method (section 4).

The assignation of each action to one of the three categories is performed by using a decision tree of the type described here under, where

$$S(a,\hat{b}) = \max_k S(a,b^k),$$

$$S(b^*,a) = \max \{S(b^k,a): b^k \neq \hat{b}\},$$

$$S(\hat{c},a) = \max_k S(c^k,a),$$

$$S(a,c^*) = \max \{S(a,c^k): c^k \neq \hat{c}\},$$

and where s,t,s',t' are thresholds to be fixed in function of the considered application and in particular by taking into account the inconveniences due to an asignment error and those resulting from any assignment to category $K^?$ (loss of time, extra costs, etc.).

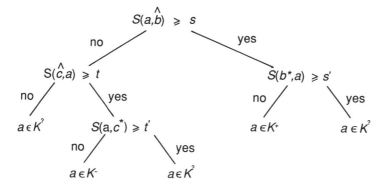

The reader will find a numerical example in Roy (1981a).

9. THE PROMETHEE METHOD (Brans and Vincke, 1985)

Just as ELECTRE III, this method consists in building a valued outranking relation, but this time trying to involve concepts and parameters which do have some physical (or economic) interpretation easily understandable by the decision-maker.

9.1 BUILDING OF THE VALUED OUTRANKING RELATION

Having assigned to each criterion a weight p_j, increasing with the importance of the criterion, the outranking degree $\pi(a,b)$ of each ordered pair of actions (a,b) is computed as follows:

$$\pi(a,b) = \frac{1}{P} \sum_{j=1}^{n} p_j F_j(a,b), \text{ where } P = \sum_{j=1}^{n} p_j,$$

and where $F_j(a,b)$ is a number between 0 and 1 which increases if $g_j(a) - g_j(b)$ is large and equals zero if $g_j(a) \le g_j(b)$. In order to estimate the $F_j(a,b)$'s, the decision-maker is offered a choice, for each criterion, between the six forms of curves presented here. According to the way his preference increases with the difference $g_j(a) - g_j(b)$, the decision maker sets, for each criterion, the form of F_j and the associated parameter(s). The parameters to be estimated have a simple interpretation since they are indifference and preference thresholds; concerning the sixth

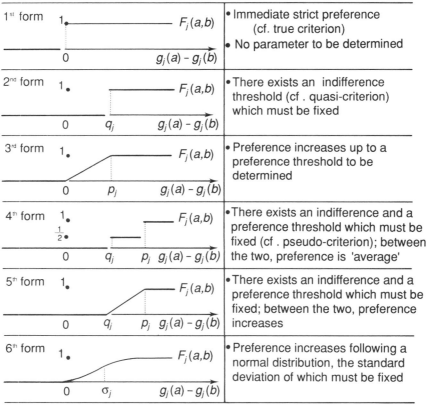

1st form	• Immediate strict preference (cf. true criterion) • No parameter to be determined
2nd form	• There exists an indifference threshold (cf . quasi-criterion) which must be fixed
3rd form	• Preference increases up to a preference threshold to be determined
4th form	• There exists an indifference and a preference threshold which must be fixed (cf . pseudo-criterion); between the two, preference is 'average'
5th form	• There exists an indifference and a preference threshold which must be fixed; between the two, preference increases
6th form	• Preference increases following a normal distribution, the standard deviation of which must be fixed

From a mathematical point of view, forms 1, 2 and 3 are obviously particular cases of form 5; it is nevertheless easier to present them separately to the decision-maker since each one corresponds to a very specific attitude when comparing $g_j(a)$ and $g_j(b)$. Other forms could obviously be introduced, but, in general, these six forms are sufficient to cover a large number of possible attitudes. $F_j(a,b)$ is thus a 'type of preference intensity' without being one in the strict sense (the term 'preference intensity' is, in fact, reserved for the case where $F_j(a,b) + F_j(b,c) = F_j(a,c)$).

The outranking degree of the PROMETHEE method is quite similar to the concordance index in the ELECTRE III method; they are even identical if all functions F_j are of form 5, except for the fact that the indifference and preference thresholds are considered as constant in the PROMETHEE method (which is a simplification but also a restriction, even though one can often go back to it by transforming the criterion). On the other hand, no discordance concept is introduced in PROMETHEE.

9.2 EXPLOITATION OF THE VALUED OUTRANKING RELATION

Just as in the previous methods, two complete preorders are built: one consists in ranking the actions following the decreasing order of numbers $\phi^+(a)$ such that

$$\phi^+(a) = \sum_{b \in A} \pi(a,b) \quad \text{(outgoing flow)},$$

and the other following the increasing order of numbers $\phi^-(a)$ such that

$$\phi^-(a) = \sum_{b \in A} \pi(b,a) \quad \text{(ingoing flow)}.$$

Their intersection yields the partial preorder of the PROMETHEE I method. The PROMETHEE II method consists in ranking the actions following the decreasing order of numbers $\phi(a)$ such that

$$\phi(a) = \phi^+(a) - \phi^-(a)$$

(generalizing the concept of qualification from the previous methods) and thus yields a unique complete preorder.

9.3 THE PROMCALC AND GAIA SOFTWARE

The PROMETHEE method gave birth to the development of a very user-friendly software called PROMCALC which includes, besides the interactive construction of functions F_j and the determination and exploitation of the valued outranking relation, a sensitivity analysis of the result with respect to weights p_j (cf. Mareschal, 1988a). The GAIA software yields, on the basis of the results determined by PROMCALC, a geometrical representation of the actions and of the criteria by application of a principal components analysis (cf. Mareschal and Brans, 1988b).

9.4 COMMENTS

The main advantage of this method is to integrate the most recent ideas of preference modelling in a very simple way. Nevertheless, as in the previous methods, what is missing is the theoretical basis which would allow a better appreciation of the assumptions on which it lies.

10. AN UNCERTAINTY OUTRANKING METHOD
   (D'Avignon and Vincke, 1988)

Besides multiple attribute utility theory, few multicriteria methods have been proposed for the treatment of situations in which the valuation of actions, for each criterion, are given under the form of probability distributions (random consequences) or frequency distributions (valuations by several experts). The method described here was motivated by a problem of valuation and comparison of projects, in which each project was judged by several experts for each criterion. This method offers the following characteristics:

● it compares actions two by two and from that point of view, can thus be classified as an outranking method;
● it preserves, for as long as possible, the distributional feature of the actions' valuations and does not replace them from the start by a unique number (mean, median, . . .) as is often the case in other approaches;
● it incorporates the concept of relative importance of the criteria and allows, for each of them, the existence of non necessarily constant thresholds.

More precisely, the data are presented as follows: each action (project) a is valued, from each point of view j, by a probability distribution $f_j(a)$; $f_j(a,x)$ represents the probability that action a takes value x for criterion j (where x is an element of a totally ordered set associated with criterion j; cf. Chapter 3).

Given two elements x and y of the ordered set associated with criterion j, we denote by $P^j(x,y)$ the preference index of x with respect to y. The estimation of functions P^j is performed by an interactive method of the PREFCALC type (cf. Chapter 4) while ensuring the following minimal properties:

$$\begin{cases} I^j(x,y) = 0 \text{ if } x \le y, \\ I^j(x,y) \le I^j(x,z) \text{ if } z \le y, \\ I^j(x,z) \ge I^j(y,z) \text{ if } x \ge y, \end{cases}$$

$$\max_{x,y} I^j(x,y) = p_j,$$

where p_j is the weight given to criterion j (we thereby consider that the preference index of the best element with respect to the worst can be used to represent the relative importance of the criterion).

The preference of an action a over an action b, for criterion j, is then random variable $H_j(a,b)$ such that

$$\mathbb{P}\,[H_j(a,b) = h] = \sum_{\{(x,y):I^j(x,y)\,=\,h\}} f_j(a,x).f_j(b,y),$$

where $0 \le h \le p_j$.

The previous formula obviously assumes independence of valuations of the actions (a reasonable assumption if the experts are not the same for the different projects); nevertheless, a more general frame can be considered, as indicated in D'Avignon and Vincke (1988).

Adopting the same approach as in the PROMETHEE method, we define the outranking of b by a through random variable

$$S(a,b) = \sum_j H_j(a,b),$$

the distribution of probability of which can be calculated on the basis of those of the $H_j(a,b)$'s.

Consequently, to each ordered pair (a,b) of actions is associated a probability distribution, defined on $[0,1]$ if $\sum_j p_j = 1$, the latter characterizing the set of advantages of a over b and taking into account the distributional aspect of the valuations, the relative importance of each criterion and the decision-maker's preferences.

Just as in the ELECTRE and PROMETHEE methods, the 'strength' and the 'weakness' of each action can then be defined as being respectively the following – eventually normalized – random variables

$$\begin{cases} S(a) = \sum_{b \ne a} S(a,b), \\ W(a) = \sum_{b \ne a} S(b,a). \end{cases}$$

The medians of these distributions yield two complete preorders which are analogous to those obtained in the ELECTRE and PROMETHEE methods. However, in order not to lose the information contained in the distributional aspect of the strength and weakness, it is suggested, in the reference given above, to associate, with these complete preorders, some indexes which take into account the more or less large overlapping of the probability distributions. For the definition of these indexes and the presentation of a numerical example, see D'Avignon and Vincke (1988).

Finally, note that if the valuations of the actions are precise numbers, one finds, as particular cases of this method:

(1) the PROMETHEE method if $P(x,y)$ is a function of the difference $x - y$;
(2) the ELECTRE II method (without discordance) if $P(x,y) = p_j$ as soon as $x > y$;
(3) aggregation by an additive function if, $\forall j$, there exists a function U^j such that $P(x,y) = U^j(x) - U^j(y)$.

CHAPTER 6
Interactive methods

This chapter is a revised version of a paper entitled 'Description and analysis of some representative interactive multicriteria procedures' by D. Vanderpooten and Ph. Vincke (1989).

1. INTRODUCTION

An interactive method consists of alternating computation steps and dialogue with the decision-maker (DM). The first computation step provides a first solution which is presented to the DM, who reacts by giving extra information about his preferences (dialogue). Injecting the latter information into the model allows a new solution to be built.

It is perhaps useful to underline the fact that any decision-aid method includes some kind of dialogue with the decision-maker, if only to define set A and the criteria; however, in order for it to be classified as an interactive method, that dialogue must be one of the principal investigation tools, meaning that the decision-maker brings a direct contribution towards the elaboration of a solution by intervening in the procedure and not only in the definition of the problem.

Many interactive methods have been proposed in the literature. We chose to describe 10 such procedures following the chronological order of their appearance: some of them have played a major part in the development of the notion of interactivity, others were selected because we felt they were representative of different routes that could be followed. Interested readers will find complementary information in Hwang and Masud (1979), White (1983), Teghem and Kunsch (1986b), Buchanan and Daellenbach (1987), Mote *et al.* (1988), Steuer and Gardiner (1990) and above all in Steuer (1986).

The notation used in this chapter was introduced in chapter 3. In order to simplify the presentation of the methods, we will essentially be working in set Z_A (the image of A in the criteria space); an element z of Z_A, proposed to the DM in the frame of an interactive method, will be called a *compromise solution*: it is in fact the image, in the space of criteria, of a compromise action a such that

$$z = (z_1,\ldots,z_n) = (g_1(a),\ldots,g_n(a)).$$

2. THE STEM METHOD
   (Benayoun *et al.*, 1971)

2.1 DESCRIPTION

The procedure consists in progressively reducing Z_A by iteratively adding constraints on the criteria values. A compromise solution z^h is computed by minimizing an augmented weighted Tchebychev norm (cf. Chapter 3, section 12) over Z_A^h, the reduced set at iteration h.

Step 0:

Determine the payoff matrix and compute the following 'normalization coefficients':

$$\lambda_j = \frac{\alpha_j}{\sum\limits_{j} \alpha_j}, \text{ where } \alpha_j = \frac{z_j^* - z_j}{|z_j^*|} \qquad (j = 1,\ldots,n).$$

   Let $Z_A^1 = Z_A$ and $h = 1$.

Step 1:

Compute a compromise solution z^h by solving the following problem:

$$\text{Min}(\mu - \sum_{j=1}^{n} \rho_j \, z_j)$$

$$\text{s.t.} \quad \mu \geq \lambda_j(z_j^{**} - z_j), \qquad (j = 1,\ldots,n).$$

$$z \in Z_A^h,$$

with $z_j^{**} = z_j^* + \epsilon_j$, where ρ_j and ϵ_j are sufficiently small positive values.

Step 2:

Present z^h to the DM.

(a) if he is satisfied with z^h, END.
(b) if not, ask him to indicate on which criterion (index) k he agrees to make a concession and which maximum amount Δ_k he accepts to concede.

Step 3:

The set of potential outcomes is reduced:

define

$$Z_A^{h+1} = \{z \in Z_A^h : z_k \geq z_k^h - \Delta_k \text{ and } z_j \geq z_j^h, \ \forall \ j \neq k\}.$$

Let $\lambda_k = 0$, $h = h+1$ and go to step 1.

2.2 COMMENTS

(1) STEM was initially proposed in the frame of multiobjective linear programming (MOLP). Our presentation suggests that the method is general enough to be adapted to other cases, including problems involving an explicit list of alternatives.
(2) In the initial MOLP presentation, the authors suggest using the following more sophisticated normalization coefficients:

$$\alpha_j = \frac{z_j^* - z_j}{|z_j^*|} \frac{1}{\|c^j\|},$$

where $\|c^j\|$ is the Euclidean norm of vector c^j (vector of the coefficients of the jth linear objective function). However, it should be pointed out that this second normalization term is scale-dependent (i.e. in general, $\|c^j\| \neq \|\beta.c^j\|$).
(3) The main drawback of the method is its 'irrevocability': when a concession is made on a criterion, it is definitively registered in the model. If the DM wants to change his mind, he is forced to start the procedure from the beginning. Similarly, as constraints $z_j \geq z_j^h$, $\forall \ j \neq k$, are irrevocable, it is not possible to reach a compromise solution which has a slightly smaller value than z_j^h (for $j \neq k$) and is much better than z^h on all other criteria.

(4) As suggested by the authors, one could relax more than one criterion in step 2. The authors point out that because of irrevocability and the fact that at least one λ_j is set to zero at each iteration, the procedure ends after at most n iterations. It should be noted that if $\lambda_j = 0$ for all j at iteration h, Z_A^{h+1} is not necessarily reduced to a unique element. In the latter case, Z_A^{h+1} cannot be explored any further by the procedure. This is another difficulty resulting from irrevocability.

(5) It is not always easy for a DM to specify Δ_k, particularly if he knows the importance of this value in the procedure and the fact that it is irrevocable. Also, it would be more natural for the DM to specify the criteria to be improved, rather than those to be relaxed.

(6) The authors point out that the DM can be helped by a sensitivity analysis, giving lower and upper bounds for variations of the criteria due to a small change in one of them. The idea of a sensitivity analysis to help the DM is essential in this type of method. However, the analysis proposed by the authors (in the MOLP case) can produce bounds which do not correspond to feasible solutions, so precautions should be taken.

(7) Calculation steps are simple. In the MOLP case, step 1 consists in solving a linear program. The construction of the payoff matrix requires n optimizations which can be performed efficiently once one notices that the only change which occurs is in the objective function. Only one optimization is needed for any subsequent iteration.

(8) STEM is certainly one of the best known interactive procedures; it also must be given credit for being the first such method proposed in the literature and having opened a fruitful field of research. Some more recent methods are probably better adapted to the needs of practitioners, but the STEM procedure was a pioneer. Moreover, we believe that most of the indicated drawbacks can be overcome by relaxing the irrevocability assumption.

3. THE METHOD OF GEOFFRION, DYER AND FEINBERG (1972)

3.1 DESCRIPTION

This method was proposed to solve multiobjective programming (MOP) problems in which A is a convex compact subset of $\mathbb{R}^p$. It is assumed that the DM wants to maximize a function $U[g_1(x),...,g_n(x)]$ which is not known explicitly but is assumed to be differentiable and concave. Roughly speaking, the DM is guided through Z_A in a way which is similar to the progression performed by classical nonlinear optimization techniques.

Step 0:

Arbitrarily choose a first compromise solution (x^1, z^1), with $z_j^1 = g_j(x^1)$ for all j. Let $h = 1$.

Step 1:

Determine the local marginal rates of substitution (or tradeoffs) λ_j^h between criteria g_j and g_1 (the reference criterion) at point z^h. By definition, we have $\lambda_j^h = (\partial U(z^h)/\partial g_j)/(\partial U(z^h)/\partial g_1)$, where $(\partial U(z^h)/\partial g_i)$ is the ith partial derivative evaluated at z^h (cf. Chapter 3, section 14). An interactive procedure to determine these tradeoffs indirectly was subsequently proposed by Dyer (1973) and is briefly described below.

Step 2:

Let $\Delta_x U[g_1(x^h),\ldots,g_n(x^h)]$ be the gradient of U at z^h.

Determine an optimal solution y^h of the following problem:

$$\text{Max } \Delta_x U[g_1(x^h),\ldots,g_n(x^h)] \cdot y,$$

$$\text{s.t. } y \in A.$$

Noting that $\Delta_x U[g_1(x^h),\ldots,g_n(x^h)] = \sum_j (\partial U(z^h)/\partial g_j).\Delta_x g_j(x^h)$ and dividing the objective function by $(\partial U(z^h)/\partial g_1)$ (which is positive), we can replace the objective function by

$$\sum_j \lambda_j^h.\Delta_x g_j(x^h).y$$

where $\Delta_x g_j(x^h)$, the gradient of g_j evaluated at x^h, can be calculated from the initial data.

$d^h = y^h - x^h$ yields locally, the best direction in which to move away from x^h.

Step 3:

Obtain from the DM a solution to the following step-size problem:

$$\text{Max } U[g_1(x^h + td^h),\dots,g_n(x^h + td^h)],$$

$$\text{s.t. } 0 \le t \le 1.$$

This is achieved through a (graphical) procedure showing the simultaneous evolutions of the n criteria as t increases from 0 to 1. By selecting the criterion vector he most prefers, the DM provides required value t^*.

Let z^{h+1} be the selected point and x^{h+1} its inverse image $(x^{h+1} = x^h + t^* d^h)$.

Step 4:

If $z^{h+1} = z^h$, then END with (x^h, z^h) as the final solution, else let $h = h + 1$ and go to step 1.

3.2 DETERMINATION OF THE λ_j^h 's

The interactive procedure proposed by Dyer (1973) allows tradeoffs λ_j^h to be assessed through a series of pairwise comparisons. The DM is asked to compare the two following solutions:

$$z^h = (z_1^h, z_2^h, \dots, z_j^h, \dots, z_n^h)$$

and

$$z'^h = (z_1^h + \Delta_1, z_2^h, \dots, z_j^h - \Delta_j, \dots, z_n^h)$$

where Δ_1 and Δ_j are small perturbations relative to z_1^h and z_j^h, respectively, but large enough to be significant.

If the DM prefers z^h to z'^h (respectively z'^h to z^h), Δ_j is decreased (respectively increased) until indifference is attained; λ_j^h is then given by Δ_j/Δ_1 (cf. Chapter 3, section 14).

3.3 COMMENTS

(1) The method of Geoffrion *et al.* is based on the very strong assumption that an implicit utility function U pre-exists, which must be optimized, and that all the answers given by the DM will be consistent with that function.

(2) The method is an adaptation of the Franke–Wolfe algorithm to the multi-objective case. This algorithm was chosen because of its robustness and its rather rapid convergence. Clearly, many other mathematical programming algorithms could be rendered interactive in a similar way.

(3) Unlike most of the methods based upon assumptions about an explicit pre-existing utility function, this procedure does not (explicitly or implicitly) eliminate any solution. Consequently, it can be used as an exploratory search process in a sort of trial-and-error approach, if prior assumptions and convergence properties are put aside.

(4) The main drawback resides in the difficulty of providing the preference information required in steps 1 and 3. It is now widely acknowledged that DM's are reluctant to specify tradeoffs. The determination of z^{h+1} (or t^*), even when graphical displays are used, becomes quite difficult when n is larger than 3 or 4.

(5) The choice of a reference criterion (cf. step 1) may turn out to be difficult. Most of the time, criteria involving financial consequences will be taken into account.

(6) Many questions must be answered at each iteration. Dyer's procedure, which allows an indirect specification of tradeoffs, requires many pairwise comparisons.

(7) The proposals obtained in step 3 may correspond to dominated points.

(8) Calculation steps are easy. In the MOLP case, step 2 reduces to a linear program. It is important to emphasize the fact that the only change at each iteration is in the objective function.

(9) The procedure of Geoffrion, Dyer and Feinberg can also be considered as a pioneering work. It gave birth to many methods which make use of other underlying optimization procedures but try to reduce the cognitive strain imposed on the DM (e.g. Sadagopan and Ravindran, 1986).

4. THE EVOLVING TARGET METHOD (Roy, 1976)

4.1 DESCRIPTION

This method iteratively determines a region of interest and a searching direction (represented by a weighting vector) which allow a proposal to be generated by minimizing an augmented weighted Tchebychev norm. This process follows a sort of trial-and-error approach.

Step 0:

Let $Z_A^1 = Z_A$ and $h = 1$.

Step 1:

Compute z^{*h}, the ideal point relative to Z_A^h and let $z^{**h} = z^{*h} + \epsilon$, where ϵ is a vector of arbitrarily small positive values.

Step 2:

Ask the DM to specify a reference point $\bar{z}^h$ corresponding to aspiration levels such that $\bar{z}_j^h \leq z*_j^h$ for all j.

Let $\lambda_j^h = 1/(z**_j^h - \bar{z}_j^h)$.

Step 3:

Calculate a compromise solution z^h by solving the following problem:

$$\text{Min}(\mu - \sum_{j=1}^{n} \rho_j \, z_j)$$

$$\text{s.t.} \quad \mu \geq \lambda_j^h (z_j^{**} - z_j), \qquad (j = 1,\ldots,n).$$

$$z \in Z_A^h,$$

where the ρ_j's are arbitrarily small positive values.

Step 4:

Present z^h to the DM:

(a) if he is satisfied with z^h, END.
(b) if not, ask him to indicate which criteria can be relaxed.

Let K be the corresponding set of criterion indices. For each $k \in K$, ask him to state the maximum Δ_k he accepts to concede.

Step 5:

The set of potential outcomes becomes:

$$Z_A^{h+1} = \{z \in Z_A : z_k \geq z_k^h - \Delta_k, \; \forall k \in K, \text{ and } z_j \geq z_j^h, \; \forall j \in \{1,\ldots,n\} \setminus K\}.$$

Let $h = h + 1$ and go to step 1.

4.2 COMMENTS

(1) The evolving target procedure can be applied to all cases, including problems involving an explicit list of alternatives.
(2) The originality of this approach lies in the fact that it refutes the assumption of a pre-existing and stable utility function. Clearly, within

this frame, the DM is not required to be consistent. He is free to change his mind. The main purpose of this type of procedure is to discover preferences through a trial-and-error approach.

(3) No mathematical convergence is required since this is a learning-oriented approach.

(4) Although not indicated in the latter description, the initial procedure envisaged possible modifications (reductions and enlargements) of the current set of alternatives. This can result from new alternatives becoming available or old ones disappearing, but also from a change of preferences which could induce the DM to explore other alternatives.

(5) The preference information required in step 4 is similar to that demanded in STEM. However, no irrevocability is required here, which makes the information easier to supply.

(6) The preference information required in step 2 is used only to guide the search within Z_A^h. We believe that such information, which increases the cognitive strain imposed on the DM, is unnecessary in a learning-oriented perspective. Indeed, it is possible to use a fixed direction of preferences (such as in STEM) and simply allow the DM to supply the information when he wants to.

(7) Calculation steps reside in the resolution of $n+1$ optimization problems at each iteration (n for building the local ideal point and one for generating the proposal).

5. THE METHOD OF ZIONTS AND WALLENIUS
   (1976, 1983)

5.1 DESCRIPTION

This method was proposed in the context of MOLP. It generates a sequence of improved extreme point solutions using local linear approximations of an implicit utility function which is assumed to be pseudo-concave.

Step 0:

Let $\Lambda^1 = \{\lambda \in R^n: \lambda_j \geq \epsilon, \sum_j \lambda_j = 1\}$ be the initial set of weighting vectors (where ϵ is a sufficiently small positive value).

Let $h = 1$.

For a $\lambda \in \Lambda^h$, solve the following linear program:

$$\text{Max} \sum_{j=1}^{n} \lambda_j \, c^j \, x,$$

$$\text{s.t.} \quad Dx \le b,$$

$$x \ge 0.$$

Let x^h be the resulting optimal solution and z^h the corresponding (nondominated) criterion vector.

Step 1:

For each nonbasic variable x_k in optimal solution (x^h, z^h), test if the introduction of x_k into the basis leads to an efficient extreme point (at worst, this test is performed by solving a linear program; cf. Zionts and Wallenius, 1980); if the test is positive, x_k is called an efficient nonbasic variable.

Determine subset M of efficient nonbasic variables, the introduction of which into the basis does not lead to solutions previously (implicitly) eliminated in step 3 or 5, and its complement N. Let indicator set $L = M$.

Step 2:

For each $x_k \epsilon L$:

(a) determine w_{jk} representing the decrease in criterion g_j due to some specified increase in x_k (these amounts are obtained from classical properties of the simplex algorithm).
(b) ask the DM if he is willing to accept the tradeoffs corresponding to simultaneous variations $w_{1k}, \ldots, w_{jk}, \ldots, w_{nk}$;

the possible answers are yes, no, and I don't know.

Step 3:

If there is no 'yes' answer then

if $L = M$, let $L = N$ and go to step 2, else END with (x^h, z^h) as the final solution;

otherwise, reduce the set of weighting vectors:

$$\Lambda^{h+1} = \{\lambda \epsilon \Lambda^h : \sum_j w_{jk} \lambda_j \le -\epsilon \text{ for each yes response and } x_k \epsilon L,$$

$$\sum_j w_{jk} \lambda_j \ge \epsilon \text{ for each no response and } x_k \epsilon L\}$$

(I don't know responses are not taken into account).

Indeed, a yes response means that the DM prefers to accept variations $w_{1k},\ldots,w_{nk}$ and thus

$$\sum_j \lambda_j \, c^j \, x^h < \sum_j \lambda_j (c^j \, x^h - w_{jk}), \text{ hence } \sum_j \lambda_j \, w_{jk} < 0.$$

Step 4:

If $\Lambda^{h+1} = \varnothing$, progressively drop the oldest active constraints until $\Lambda^{h+1} \neq \varnothing$.

For a $\lambda \in \Lambda^{h+1}$, solve the linear program of step 0. Denote the corresponding solution as (x^{h+1}, z^{h+1}).

Step 5:

Ask the DM to indicate which of z^h and z^{h+1} he prefers:

(a) if z^h is chosen, END with (x^h, z^h). In fact, one could find better solutions but which are nonextreme points.
(b) if z^{h+1} is chosen, modify Λ^{h+1} by adding constraint

$$\sum_j (z_j^{h+1} - z_j^h) \, \lambda_j \geq \epsilon.$$

Let $h = h + 1$ and go to step 1.

5.2 COMMENTS

(1) The method of Zionts and Wallenius is restricted to MOLP problems. However, some extensions have been proposed in the multiple objective integer programming and the discrete case (cf. Zionts, 1977, 1989).
(2) The method is based upon the very strong assumption that an underlying (pseudo-concave) utility function pre-exists and that the DM's answers are consistent with it. Because of some difficulties due to this assumption (e.g. in step 4), the authors decided, in a somewhat arbitrary way, to discard the oldest information.
(3) The compromise solutions provided by the method are always extreme points. This is a consequence of using Theorem 1 (Chapter 3, section 12) to characterize nondominated points. Clearly, good compromise solutions may correspond to nonextreme points.

(4) The acceptation of a tradeoff in step 3 involves a constraint in the set of weighting vectors. However, using a weighting vector in step 4 which belongs to the reduced set may result in a solution which does not match the accepted tradeoff (cf. De Samblanckx *et al.*, 1982). In other words, if an increase on a criterion is proposed and accepted in the tradeoff, it can easily happen that the following solution shows a decrease on that criterion. Even if this is not really an error, it could be misleading for the DM.

(5) Questions concerning tradeoffs are generally considered to be complicated. This is why, in a more recent description (1983), the authors proposed to replace tradeoffs by pairwise comparisons between the current and each of the adjacent efficient extreme solutions. However, tradeoffs cannot always be avoided (e.g. because the DM may reject an adjacent point and accept the limited corresponding tradeoff). The resulting method seems easier to use.

(6) The DM must answer many questions.

(7) Many calculations must be performed. Except for the linear program which is used at each iteration to generate a new proposal, most of these calculations are necessary for the identification of the efficient nonbasic variables.

6. THE METHOD OF VINCKE (1976b)

6.1 DESCRIPTION

This method, proposed in the context of MOLP, performs an interactive sensitivity analysis using classical simplex properties.

Step 0:

Identical to step 0 of STEM.

Step 1:

Identical to step 1 of STEM, with $Z_A^h = Z_A$.

Step 2:

z^h is presented to the DM:

(a) if he is satisfied with z^h, END.

(b) if not, he is successively asked the following questions:

— which criterion do you want to improve?
— do you agree to accept a concession on a criterion? Which criterion?
— do you agree to relax a constraint? Which constraint?
— do you want to be more restrictive on a constraint? Which constraint?

If the DM is interested in a given perturbation, he is made aware of the corresponding consequences (see below: sensitivity analysis); if he accepts these consequences, a new compromise z^{h+1} is determined (see below). Let $h = h+1$ and go to step 2.

6.2 SENSITIVITY ANALYSIS

The linear program yielding the successive compromise solutions can be written as follows:

$$\text{Min } (\mu - \sum_{j=1}^{n} \rho_j \, c_j \, x + \sum_{j=1}^{n} M_j \, v_j),$$

$$\text{s.t.} \qquad D_i x + t_i^1 = b_i, \; \forall \; i,$$

$$\mu + \lambda_j \, c^j \, x - t_j^2 + v_j = \lambda_j \, z_j^{**}, \qquad (j = 1, \ldots, n),$$

$$z_j - c^j \, x = 0, \qquad (j = 1, \ldots, n),$$

$$x \geq 0, \; t_i^1 \geq 0, \; t_j^2 \geq 0, \; v_j \geq 0,$$

where $z_j^{**} = z_j^* + \epsilon_j$, ρ_j and ϵ_j are sufficiently small positive values, the M_j's are arbitrarily large positive values, the t_i^1's and t_j^2's are slack variables and the v_j's are artificial variables; the z_j's are unrestricted.

The perturbations proposed in step 2 can be seen as modifications of z_j^{**} or b_i. Noticing that the basic variables at the beginning of the procedure are t_i^1, v_j and z_j, the consequences on the criteria of the proposed perturbations can be simply read, in the simplex tableau, in columns t_i^1 and v_j and in rows z_j (cf. shadow prices in classical linear programming). Moreover, it is easy to calculate the minimal value of the perturbation leading to a change of basis, i.e. the range of validity of the sensitivity analysis.

6.3 DETERMINATION OF z^{h+1}

Following the information received from the sensitivity analysis, the DM may accept the proposed perturbation and choose its magnitude (if he refuses it, the procedure goes to the following question). If he does, z^{h+1} is determined by updating the last simplex tableau. This is achieved by changing the values of the basic variables or possibly by performing one dual simplex iteration if the DM chose the maximal magnitude of the perturbation in its range of validity.

6.4 COMMENTS

(1) The method of Vincke is restricted to MOLP problems.
(2) It follows a learning-oriented perspective. There is no irrevocability: going back is always possible.
(3) There is no mathematical convergence involved, which is natural in a learning-oriented approach.
(4) The possibility of modifying the set of alternatives under consideration is explicitly included in the method: the DM can change the constraints during the procedure.
(5) The method performs an interactive sensitivity analysis. This amounts to saying that the DM must approximately know his region of interest. More precisely, the first compromise solution z^1 should not be too far from that region.
(6) The method necessitates a constant dialogue with the DM. The information required is mainly qualitative.
(7) All calculation steps are particularly simple. After the n linear programs which are solved in order to determine the ideal point and another linear program to compute the first compromise solution, at most one dual simplex iteration is required at each iteration.

7. THE REFERENCE POINT METHOD (Wierzbicki, 1980, 1982)

7.1 DESCRIPTION

This approach is a general framework rather than a specific method. The DM is iteratively asked to specify aspiration levels (or reference points). Best approximations of these points are calculated by using an 'achievement scalarizing function' s.

Step 0:

Give the DM some preliminary information such as the payoff matrix. Choose a weighting vector λ. Let $h = 1$.

Step 1:

Ask the DM to specify his aspiration levels:

$$\bar{z}^h = (\bar{z}_1^h, \dots, \bar{z}_n^h), \quad (\bar{z}^h \in z).$$

Step 2:

Let z^h be the optimal solution of the following program:

$$\text{Min } s(z, \bar{z}_h, \lambda),$$

$$\text{s.t. } z \in Z_A.$$

If the DM is satisfied with z^h then END else let $h = h + 1$ and go to step 1.

For the choice of s, see the comments following.

7.2 COMMENTS

(1) The reference point approach can be applied to any case, including problems involving an explicit list of alternatives.

(2) The approach used here is based on aspiration levels and is thus different from the utility maximization framework. Intuitively, if the aspiration levels are not attainable, s generates a nondominated point closest to the desired levels. If the aspiration levels are attainable with a surplus, s generates a nondominated point while making the best possible use of that surplus. The author calls this a quasi-satisficing framework.

(3) In accordance with (2), the achievement scalarizing function is chosen in a way which ensures that compromise solutions correspond to nondominated points. The properties of these functions, along with some examples, are given in Wierzbicki (1986).

(4) This approach follows a learning-oriented perspective.

(5) Clearly, aspiration levels can be specified rather easily by a DM at the beginning of the procedure. However, it is sometimes difficult for him to iteratively provide new ones. Even if z^h and $\bar{z}^h$ give indications for setting $\bar{z}^{h+1}$, the relationship is not clear enough to stimulate a natural specification.

(6) The basic procedure can be extended in many ways. Relevant dual information can be presented to the DM, several reference points can be used at each iteration, and so on. A direct extension, proposed by Wierzbicki, consists in using n additional perturbed reference points:

$$\bar{z}_{hj} = \bar{z}^h + d_h . e_j \qquad (j = 1, \dots, n),$$

where d_h is the distance between reference point $\bar{z}^h$ and the corresponding nondominated point (cf. step 2), and e_j is the jth unit vector. At the expense of extra calculations, these perturbed reference points give a description of the set of nondominated points in the neighbourhood of $\bar{z}^h$.

8. THE METHOD OF STEUER AND CHOO (1983)

8.1 DESCRIPTION

The procedure provides samples of progressively smaller subsets of nondominated points. These samples consist of P ($\approx n$) representative points, generated by using an augmented weighted Tchebychev norm, from which the DM is required to select one as his most preferred.

Step 0:

Calculate the ideal point z^* and let $z^{**} = z^* + \epsilon$, where ϵ is a vector of arbitrarily small positive values.

Let $\Lambda^1 = \{\lambda \in \mathbb{R}^n : \lambda_j \in [0,1], \sum_j \lambda_j = 1\}$ be the initial set of weighting vectors.

Let $h = 1$.

Step 1:

Randomly generate a large number ($\approx 50n$) of weighting vectors from Λ^h.

Filter this set to obtain a fixed number ($2n$ is proposed) of representative weighting vectors (for the filtering procedure, see comment 4 below).

Step 2:

For each representative weighting vector λ, solve the following corresponding augmented weighted Tchebychev program:

$$\text{Min}(\mu - \sum_{j=1}^{n} \rho_j \, z_j)$$

$$\text{s.t.} \quad \mu \geq \lambda_j(z_j^{**} - z_j), \qquad (j = 1,...,n).$$

$$z \in Z_A,$$

where the ρ_j's are sufficiently small positive values.

Filter the $2P$ resulting nondominated points to obtain P solutions.

Step 3:

Present the P compromise solutions to the DM and ask him to select the one he most prefers. Let z^h be the selected point.

Step 4

(a) If $h = t$ then END with z^h as the preferred solution (where t is a prespecified number of iterations); else

(b) Let λ^h be the weighting vector which generated z^h in step 2.

Its components are given by:

$$\lambda_j^h = \frac{1}{z_j^{**} - z_j^{h}} \left[\sum_{l=1}^{n} \frac{1}{z_l^{**} - z_l^{h}} \right]^{-1} (j = 1,\ldots,n).$$

Determine the reduced set of weighting vectors:

$$\Lambda^{h+1} = \{\lambda \in \mathbb{R}^n : \lambda_j \in [l_j, u_j], \sum_j \lambda_j = 1\},$$

where

$$[l_j, u_j] = \begin{cases} [0, r^h] & \text{if } \lambda_j^h \leq r^h/2, \\ [1 - r^h, 1] & \text{if } \lambda_j^h \geq 1 - r^h/2, \\ [\lambda_j^h - r^h/2, \ \lambda_j^h + r^h/2] & \text{otherwise,} \end{cases}$$

in which r^h is a prespecified 'convergence factor' r raised to the hth power.

Let $h = h + 1$ and go to step 1.

8.2 COMMENTS

(1) The method of Steuer and Choo can be applied to any case, including problems involving an explicit list of alternatives.

(2) No assumption is made about an explicit utility function.

(3) The DM can change his mind, but only to a certain extent because of the monotonic reduction of the set of weighting vectors.

(4) The filtering procedure used in steps 1 and 2 is described in Steuer and Harris (1980). This is an attractive way of presenting dispersed, and thus representative, compromise solutions.

(5) The main drawback of the method is that many technical parameters (P,t,r) must be prespecified without there being any intuitive meaning. The authors propose 'rules of thumb' to set these values.

(6) The preference information required from the DM is qualitative and rather natural (step 3). However, it may become difficult to obtain as the number of criteria increases.

(7) The stopping rule of step 4(a) is somewhat artificial. It is significant that, in a more recent version, Steuer (1986) suggests letting the DM end the procedure whenever he wishes, i.e. whether $h < t$ or $h > t$. In fact, we believe that parameter t should be ignored.

(8) Many calculations take place at each iteration. Except for the initial optimizations to compute z^*, $2P$ step 2-type problems must be solved at each iteration (plus 2 filtering procedures). This drawback results directly from a desire to ensure dispersion and representativeness of the proposed solutions.

9. THE METHOD OF KORHONEN AND LAAKSO (1986)

9.1 DESCRIPTION

In this procedure, the DM is iteratively asked to specify aspiration levels from which a curve of nondominated points is derived. This curve is graphically presented to the DM, who is required to indicate the solution he most prefers.

Step 0:

Choose an arbitrary point z^0 and a weighting vector λ.

Let $h = 1$.

Step 1:

Ask the DM to specify his aspiration levels (or reference point):

$$\bar{z}^h = (\bar{z}^h_1, \dots, \bar{z}^h_n), \quad (\bar{z}^h \in z).$$

Take $d^h = \bar{z}^h - z^{h-1}$ as the new reference direction.

Step 2:

Solve the following parametric problem:

$$\text{Min } s(z,y,\lambda),$$

$$\text{s.t. } y = z^{h-1} + t \ d^h,$$

$$z \epsilon Z_A,$$

where t is increased from zero to infinity.

In this step, each point y is projected onto the nondominated frontier of Z_A (if s is properly chosen). This results in a curve of nondominated points. See comment 4 for the choice of s.

Step 3:

Present the curve graphically to the DM displaying a diagram similar to one used in the Geoffrion, Dyer and Feinberg method.
    Ask the DM to select the compromise solution he most prefers.

Let z^h be that point.

Step 4:

(a) If $z^h = z^{h-1}$, check some optimality conditions (cf. Korhonen and Laakso, 1986). If they are satisfied, END with z^h as the final solution, else a new reference direction d^{h+1} is identified by the optimality test; let $h = h + 1$ and go to step 2.
(b) If $z^h \neq z^{h-1}$, let $h = h + 1$ and go to step 1.

9.2 COMMENTS

(1) The method of Korhonen and Laakso can be applied to any case, including problems involving an explicit list of alternatives.
(2) Optimality conditions are based on the assumption that the DM's utility function is pseudo-concave. It should be noted that this assumption is used only when those conditions must be checked.
(3) The procedure mainly follows a learning-oriented perspective. However, it also aims at strengthening the DM's confidence in the final prescription.
(4) Any classical scalarizing function with convenient nondominance properties can be chosen as s. Using an augmented weighted Tchebychev norm, the problem of step 2 becomes:

$$\text{Min } (\mu - \sum_{j=1}^{n} \rho_j \, z_j)$$

$$\text{s.t.} \quad \mu \geq \quad \lambda_j \, (z_j^{h-1} + t\mathrm{d}_j - z_j), \qquad (j = 1, \ldots, n),$$

$$z \in Z_A,$$

with t increased from zero to infinity.

(5) Preference information required from the DM consists of aspiration levels. The possible difficulties which can arise from using such information were discussed in section 7.2.

(6) The way in which weighting vector λ is chosen is not indicated by the authors. Clearly, the nondominated curve resulting from step 2 is greatly influenced by this choice (in some extreme cases, this curve can reduce to the current point).

(7) Calculation steps depend strongly upon the problem at hand. In the MOLP case, classical parametric programming can be applied. In other cases, several optimizations must be performed (at each iteration) for specific values of t.

10. THE METHOD OF JACQUET-LAGRÈZE, MEZIANI AND SLOWINSKI (1987)

10.1 DESCRIPTION

In this method, a global utility function is interactively built taking into account a subset of alternatives. It is then applied to the initial set in order to derive a solution.

Step 0:

Determine the payoff matrix, the ideal point z^* and the nadir point $\underline{z}$.

Step 1:

Generate representative points by the following procedure:

Let $\lambda_j = 1/(z_j^* - \underline{z}_j)$ for all j and solve the weighted Tchebychev problem to generate first point z^0.

Considering q interior points $z^0 - (r/q)(z^0 - z)$ $(r = 1, \ldots, q)$, for each point solve the following n problems $(k = 1, \ldots, n)$:

$$\text{Max } z_k,$$

$$\text{s.t. } z \geq z^0 - (r/q)(z^0 - z),$$

$$z \in Z_A.$$

This results in a sample of $q \times n$ weakly nondominated points (q is arbitrarily chosen).

Step 2:

Ask the DM to estimate piecewise-linear marginal utility functions, u_j for each criterion g_j. This is achieved through interactive cycles of:

— direct estimations of u_j at some breakpoints using graphical displays.
— indirect estimations based upon ordinal regression methods (cf. Jacquet-Lagrèze and Siskos, 1982b). In this case, the DM is first asked to rank the alternatives selected in step 1.

The general utility function is given by: $U(z) = \sum_j u_j(z_j)$.

Step 3:

Determine the final solution by extrapolating U over Z_A:

$$\text{Max } U(z),$$

$$\text{s.t. } z \in Z_A.$$

10.2 COMMENTS

(1) The method of Jacquet-Lagrèze *et al.* can be applied to any case, including problems involving an explicit list of alternatives.

(2) In this method, the interaction is primarily directed toward the construction of a local utility function (step 2). Unlike the other interactive procedures, the DM is presented with only one proposal (step 3) which is to be considered as the final solution.

(3) No irrevocability is imposed as long as the assessment is not completed, i.e. the DM is free to adjust his utility function.

(4) The utility function which is assessed from a subset of alternatives is assumed to remain valid with respect to the initial set. This assumption is all the more strong as the DM cannot react against the final solution.

(5) The generation procedure of step 1 aims at generating several dispersed alternatives. It can produce weakly nondominated points.

Moreover, some nondominated points (such as those for which some coordinates are smaller than the corresponding coordinates of the nadir point) cannot be generated. In order to overcome these technical difficulties and also to ensure a better representation, filtering techniques can be applied.

(6) Concerning preference information, the graphical displays of marginal utility functions are usually well accepted by the DM. The direct specification of a ranking on a subset of alternatives (step 2) is not easy. However, a very interesting feature is the fact that the DM can appreciate the impact of a modification of his ranking on the marginal utility functions and conversely.

(7) As indicated by the authors and because of the specificity of this approach, only the calculations directly involving the DM must be considered (steps 0, 1 and 3 can be performed independently). The calculations of step 2 are quite simple. Each ordinal regression is achieved by solving a linear program.

11. THE METHOD OF VANDERPOOTEN
(Vanderpooten and Vincke, 1989)

11.1 DESCRIPTION

This method proposes pairwise comparisons between the current preferred alternative and another one which represents a potential improvement. The response of the DM is analysed in order to derive a region of interest from which a new proposal may emerge.

Step 0:

Let $\bar{z}^0 = z^{*0} + \epsilon$, where z^{*0} is the ideal point relative to Z_A and $\lambda^1 > 0$ is an arbitrary weighting vector (e.g. determined as in STEM).

Compute a first compromise solution by solving:

$$\text{Min } s(z, \bar{z}^0, \lambda^1),$$

$$\text{s.t. } z \in Z_A.$$

Let $\bar{Z}_A^0 = Z_A$ and $h = 1$.

Step 1:

Considering z^{h-1}, ask the DM to indicate which criteria should be improved. J is the current set of criterion indices.

(a) if $J = \varnothing$, END with z^{h-1} as the final solution.
(b) if not, let the new region of interest be

$$Z_A^h = \{z \in \bar{Z}_A^{h-1}: \; z_j \geq z_j^{h-1}, \; \forall \; j \in J\}.$$

Let $\bar{z}^h = z^{*h} + \epsilon$, where z^{*h} is the ideal point relative to Z_A^h.

Step 2:

Calculate a new compromise solution by solving:

$$\text{Min } s(z, \bar{z}^h, \lambda^h),$$

$$\text{s.t. } z \in Z_A^h.$$

Step 3:

Ask the DM which of z^{h-1} and z^h he most prefers.
(a) if z^h is chosen, determine a first approximation of the next region of interest:

$$\bar{Z}_A^h = \{z \in Z_A : z_j \geq z_j^{h-1}, \; \forall \; j \in J\}.$$

(b) if z^{h-1} is chosen, ask the DM to indicate which criteria (the values of which have decreased) are responsible for this judgement. Let K be the corresponding set of criterion indices. The first approximation of the next region of interest is given by:

$$\bar{Z}_A^h = \{z \in Z_A : z_k \geq z_k^h, \; \forall k \in K\}.$$

Let $z^h = z^{h-1}$.

Step 4:

Let $\bar{z}^h = \bar{z}^{*h} + \epsilon$, where $\bar{z}^{*h}$ is the ideal point relative to $\bar{Z}_A^h$.

The new weighting vector (preference direction) λ^{h+1} is determined by:

$$\lambda_j^{h+1} = \frac{1}{\bar{z}_j^h - z_j^h} \qquad (j = 1, \ldots, n).$$

Let $h = h + 1$ and go to step 1.

11.2 COMMENTS

(1) The method of Vanderpooten can be applied to any case, including problems involving an explicit list of alternatives.

(2) The method was designed in a learning-oriented perspective. However, by temporarily preserving information obtained from the last iteration (step 3), it also aims at directing this learning through locally consistent proposals.

(3) Except for the restriction indicated in 2, previous information is omitted in order to allow trial-and-error explorations and changes of mind. Consequently, as usual with learning-oriented procedures, new proposals may be in contradiction with previous ones (which is not necessarily unreasonable).

(4) Although not indicated in the description above, the method allows the DM to set minimal requirements (reservation) levels if he wishes to avoid subsequent contradictions. It should be noted that such levels are introduced only when the DM experiences a contradiction, i.e. when his preferences become more structured.

(5) Any classical scalarizing function with convenient nondominance properties could be chosen as s. An augmented weighted Tchebychev norm is suggested by the author.

(6) The preference information required is qualitative. Moreover, some questions follow logically from the DM's answers (step 1(b) and step 3(b)).

(7) Calculation steps reside in the resolution of $n + 1$ optimization problems at each iteration (n for constructing the local ideal point and one for generating the proposal).

12. GENERAL COMMENTS

Although each procedure has specific features, a basic distinction should be made concerning the underlying approaches. Two main conceptions, highly related to various perceptions of the decision process and the way to improve it (cf. Vanderpooten, 1989, for further details), should be distinguished to classify interactive procedures:

— a search-oriented conception

— a learning-oriented conception.

Our chronological description highlights an evolution from search-oriented methods to learning-oriented procedures. It should also be noted that the most recent methods aim at including both aspects.

We now briefly discuss some critical points for the choice (or the design) of an interactive procedure. A summary of the important features of each method presented is also given in section 13.

12.1 CALCULATION STEPS

In many cases, it is useless to introduce sophisticated calculation steps. Unlike other multicriteria approaches, no definitive aggregation must be performed. Consequently, the choice of a scalarizing function (weighted sum, distance,...) should preferably lead to simple formulas and calculations; indeed, that choice is much less important than the quality of the dialogue with the DM. Moreover, in order to be operational and accepted by the DMs, such procedures must involve reasonable computation times.

However, the choice of a scalarizing function is not completely arbitrary. Some desirable technical requirements (e.g. nondominance properties) should also guide this choice. Theoretical work indicating the properties of classical scalarizing functions (e.g. in Wierzbicki, 1986) is quite helpful in this respect.

12.2 PREFERENCE INFORMATION AND DIALOGUE

Preference information is used to offer potentially improved compromise solutions to the DM. From that viewpoint, the more information considered, the better. However, one should keep in mind that the main purpose is to support the DM and not the procedure.

Consequently, qualitative questions will be preferred to quantitative ones. First, in many cases, DMs are unable to provide quantitative information. Second, it is in fact useless to require too much precision in the answers if it is accepted that the DM might change his mind. Furthermore, the DM must be prepared to answer a series of questions at each iteration. If the cognitive strain is too high for each question, he may be tempted to maintain his previous answers. Such anchoring effects should be avoided, above all in a learning-oriented perspective.

Finally, it is important that the DM understand the reasons for which questions arise. There must be a dialogue in order for questions to logically follow the DM's answers. Only then will the procedure be perceived as exhibiting intelligent behaviour.

12.3 SUPPORT TO THE DM

In relation with the former point, support to the DM is one of the most important aspects of an interactive method. The role of such a method is not to decide for the DM, but to enlighten him on his problem: what is possible, what are the consequences of a certain choice, how can an aspect be improved, and so on. The procedure should bring the DM extra information.

First of all, proposals must be presented in a convenient form. Graphical displays are valuable in this respect. Additional information resulting from a sensitivity analysis, for example, should also be developed.

12.4 CONVERGENCE OF INTERACTIVE PROCEDURES

The problem of convergence is essential because it is the origin of several restrictions and drawbacks of many methods, such as:

— the irrevocability of decisions;

— the assumption that the DM's answers are always consistent with a utility function;

— the consideration of only a subset of feasible solutions (extreme points).

The purpose of an interactive method is essentially to find a 'satisfactory compromise solution'. The concept of optimality has no validity if it is accepted that learning of preferences should be supported by an interactive procedure: a solution could be rejected at the beginning and finally be accepted because of the evolution of the DM's preference structure. Consequently, the procedure should not be ended because of any convergence test, but only if the DM is satisfied with a solution or when he gets the feeling he has enough information about his problem.

Although mathematical convergence is of no interest, an interactive procedure should also aim at guiding the DM's search for improved solutions. It should be clear that this improvement refers only to the current state of the DM's preference structure. Finally, we believe that the future of interactive procedures lies in trying to reconcile search and learning.

13. SUMMARY OF THE CHARACTERISTICS OF THE METHODS DESCRIBED

Methods	Assumption of existence of a utility function	Field of application	Learning aspect	Restriction of the set of solutions
STEM (1971)	No	All cases	No	Yes
Geoffrion *et al.* (1972)	Yes	MOP	Yes	No
Roy (1976)	No	All cases	Yes	No
Zionts and Wallenius (1976)	Yes	MOLP (extending)	Partially	Yes
Vincke (1976b)	No	MOLP	Yes	No
Wierzbicki (1980)	No	All cases	Yes	No
Steuer and Choo (1983)	No	All cases	Partially	Yes
Korhonen and Laakso (1986)	Yes (Partially used)	All cases	Yes	No
Jacquet-Lagrèze *et al.* (1987)	No	All cases	Yes	No
Vanderpooten (1988)	No	All cases	Yes	No

Methods	Mathematical convergence	Number of questions to the DM	Difficulty of the questions	Number of calculations (for MOLP)
STEM (1971)	Yes	Few	Rather simple	Few
Geoffrion *et al.* (1972)	Yes	Many	Difficult	Few
Roy (1976)	No	Rather few	Rather simple	Rather few
Zionts and Wallenius (1976)	Yes	Many	Rather difficult	Many
Vincke (1976b)	No	Many	Simple	Very few
Wierzbicki (1980)	No	Few	Rather simple	Few
Steuer and Choo (1983)	Yes	Few	Rather simple	Many
Korhonen and Laakso (1986)	Yes	Rather few	Rather simple	Rather few
Jacquet-Lagrèze *et al.* (1987)	No	Few	Rather simple	Few
Vanderpooten (1988)	No	Few	Simple	Rather few

CHAPTER 7
Miscellaneous questions

1. ELEMENTARY MULTICRITERIA METHODS

We call 'elementary' those methods which immediately come to mind when one is confronted with a multicriteria aggregation problem: they are in fact quite often used in practice. However, because of their simplicity, they often risk hiding some important aspects of the problem at hand.

1.1 THE WEIGHTED AVERAGE METHOD

The most 'elementary' method is certainly the one which consists in building a global preference structure {P,I} as follows:

$$
\begin{cases}
a\mathrm{P}b \text{ iff } \sum_{j=1}^{n} p_j g_j(a) > \sum_{j=1}^{n} p_j g_j(b), \\
\\
a\mathrm{I}b \text{ iff } \sum_{j=1}^{n} p_j g_j(a) = \sum_{j=1}^{n} p_j g_j(b).
\end{cases}
$$

We saw (Chapter 3, section 14) that in such a case, 'weights' p_j represent, up to a factor, substitution rates between criteria. This method thus assumes that all criteria can be expressed in identical units and that differences between values on different criteria are comparable and can compensate each other. Furthermore, this aggregation does not help clarify the more or less conflicting character of the criteria, as can be seen by the following example.

g_j	p_j	a	b	c	d
g_1	1/2	100	50	200	0
g_2	1/2	100	50	0	100

In this example,

$$\begin{cases} \sum_j p_j g_j(a) = 100 > \sum_j p_j g_j(b) = 50, \\ \sum_j p_j g_j(c) = 100 > \sum_j p_j g_j(d) = 50; \end{cases}$$

ordered pairs (a,b) and (c,d) are treated in exactly the same way by the method, although a dominates b while there is a serious conflict between the two criteria for the comparison of c and d.

The preference structure obtained by this method is a complete preorder structure, as long as the g_j's are true criteria. If they are quasi- or pseudo-criteria, the definition of P and I must be modified and these two relations are no longer transitive (see Roy and Bouyssou, 1987c).

To conclude, we would be tempted to say that the weighted average method is relevant when the criteria represent different aspects of the same global characteristic, which can be expressed in the same units and are totally compensatory (a large difference on one criterion can be compensated by several small ones on the others), the classical example being the different components of a global cost (but is this still a multicriteria problem?). Finally, let us note that it is also this method which is applied, in general, to evaluate students (on this subject, see Scharlig, 1985, Chapter 6).

1.2 THE LEXICOGRAPHIC METHOD

This method assumes one has at hand an order of importance of the criteria and that the decision-maker agrees to completely neglect the $(n - k)$ least important criteria if the k first ones allow him to reach a conclusion (k may be equal to 1). More precisely, the method consists in building a global preference structure {P,I} as follows:

$$\begin{cases} a\mathrm{P}b \text{ iff there exists a criterion } j \text{ such that } g_j(a) > g_j(b) \\ \qquad \text{and if } g_l(a) = g_l(b) \text{ for any criterion } l \text{ which is} \\ \qquad \text{more important than } j, \\ \\ a\mathrm{I}b \text{ iff } g_l(a) = g_l(b), \forall\, l. \end{cases}$$

The reader will find a complete axiomatic study of this method in Fishburn (1974a). When the g_j's are true criteria, the obtained preference structure is a complete preorder structure. If they are quasi-criteria, some circuits may appear in relation P; it is therefore necessary to modify the definition of P and I if the aim is to obtain a global preference structure which has interesting properties: this question was, among others, studied by Pirlot and Vincke (1991). If the g_j's are pseudo-criteria, the definition of P and I raises difficult questions which were put forward by Roy and Bouyssou (1987c).

Let us also note that the lexicographic method can be seen as a particular case of the weighted average method: it is sufficient to allot weights to criteria in such a way that no difference in favour of a on one criterion can be compensated by any accumulation of differences in favour of b on the less important criteria.

To conclude, the method seems only to be interesting in very special cases because of assumptions made on the relative importance of the criteria.

1.3 THE SUM OF RANKS (BORDA'S METHOD)

Another form of weighted average consists in taking $p_j = 1$, ∀ j and replacing $g_j(a)$ by

$$(|A| + 1) - r_j(a),$$

where $r_j(a)$ is the rank of a for criterion j, i.e. the position held by a when the actions are ranked following the decreasing order of function g_j's values. This is equivalent in fact to defining

$$\begin{cases} a\mathrm{P}b \text{ iff} \sum_j r_j(a) < \sum_j r_j(b), \\ a\mathrm{I}b \text{ iff} \sum_j r_j(a) = \sum_j r_j(b). \end{cases}$$

This method was proposed (under a slightly more general form) in 1770, by Jean-Charles de Borda, to the Académie des Sciences de Paris, for the aggregation of n rankings into a unique ranking. It is indeed the first method which comes to mind when the data of the multicriteria problem are given in an ordinal form. Nevertheless, summing the ranks amounts to treating the data in a cardinal way since differences between the ranks on different criteria may compensate each other.

The sum of ranks, a particular case of the weighted average, can be seen as the ancestor of multiple attribute utility theory (on this subject, see Vansnick, 1986a).

1.4 THE MAJORITY RULE (CONDORCET'S METHOD)

In 1785, the marquis de Condorcet, reopening the problem studied by Borda, proposed to declare aPb when the number of criteria (voters) for which a is better than b is larger than the number of criteria for which b is better than a. The relation obtained thereby is obviously not necessarily transitive; the 'paradox of Condorcet' is the case for which a circuit is present in relation P, which occurs, for example, when there are three criteria respectively yielding rankings abc, bca and cab.

The difference with the previous method is that the greater or lesser proximity between a and b in the rankings according to the different criteria doesn't intervene at all in the final result: all compensations between differences have disappeared.

Condorcet's method can be seen as the ancestor of outranking methods (on this subject, see Vansnick, 1986a).

1.5 ADJUSTMENT METHODS

To end this section devoted to elementary multicriteria methods, we must mention the approach consisting in seeking a preference structure 'at minimum distance' from the set of preference structures defined by the n criteria: this obviously allows one to choose whichever final preference structure one wishes. The definition of the 'distance' is arbitrary: the one most commonly used is without any doubt symmetric difference because it leads to relatively simple algorithms.

Adjustment problems bring multicriteria problems back to combinatorial optimization problems: from that point of view, they raise exciting theoretical and algorithmic questions: see, for example, Bernard and Besson (1971), Monjardet (1973), Barthelemy and Monjardet (1981).

From a decision-aid point of view, these methods may seem slightly artificial owing to the fact that they replace the multicriteria problem by a mathematical problem the interpretation of which is not clear to the decision-maker.

2. ABOUT INTERCRITERION INFORMATION

As soon as one wishes to enrich the dominance relation, it becomes necessary to introduce some information about the way in which the criteria interact: in this direction, we go into three important notions here under: *compensation*, *weights*, and *independence*.

2.1 COMPENSATION BETWEEN CRITERIA

Choosing a multicriteria aggregation method is in fact equivalent to choosing a type of 'compensation' between the criteria. Up to now, this fundamental concept hasn't been studied very thoroughly although it is quite an important tool if the aim is to advance toward axiomatics and a classification of multicriteria methods, as can be seen in the work of Fishburn (1976a) and of Bouyssou (1984a, 1986). Intuitively, the compensation aspect of a method is the more or less great possibility to counterbalance a disadvantage on one criterion by an advantage on another. More precisely, no entirely satisfactory general definition exists yielding an important research subject. The reader will find in Bouyssou (1986) some proposals of precise definitions, along with the description of the context to set in order for these definitions to make sense.

The lexicographic method and the 'concordance' part of the ELECTRE I and II methods are examples of non-compensatory methods. By defining a concept of 'generalized non-compensation', Bouyssou and Vansnick (1986) also took into account the 'discordance' part of the ELECTRE methods.

The implications of non-compensation were exploited by Vansnick (1986b) in the TACTIC method; in particular, non-compensation makes it easy to define a 'more important than' relation in the set of criteria coalitions (see following section).

Conversely, a method which is not non-compensatory is called compensatory. By replacing the corresponding conditions, different degrees of compensation are obtained (cf. Bouyssou, 1986). The additive model of multiple attribute utility theory is a typical example of a strongly compensatory method.

A non-compensatory method requires, as intercriterion information, a relative importance relation between criteria and a discordance set. It favours 'well balanced' actions to the detriment of actions which are very good with respect to some criteria and very bad with respect to others. Nevertheless, it often happens that when a person is confronted with an aggregation of criteria, he uses compensatory-like reasoning, at least when small preference differences are at stake. It therefore seems interesting to have at hand some methods which are intermediary between non-compensatory (of the 'outranking' type) and compensatory (of the 'multiple attribute utility' type): a study of such methods along with some very interesting theoretical results can be found in Bouyssou (1986).

2.2 WEIGHTS OF CRITERIA

The relative importance of the criteria is a crucial piece of information. Most methods translate this relative importance into numbers, which are often called 'weights'. It must, however, be emphasized that the interpretation of these weights isn't always straightforward and strongly depends upon the use which is made of them. One must therefore be very cautious when using the same weights in different methods to compare results: such a comparison may be totally void of sense.

In the weighted average method, 'weights' are in fact constants of scale (if one changes the unit in which a criterion is expressed, its weight changes). We saw (Chapter 3, section 14) that they are equal, up to a factor, to the substitution rates allowing the differences of preferences relative to different criteria to be expressed on the same scale. In such a case, the estimation of weights is equivalent to that of substitution rates: the questions to be asked are in terms of 'gain with respect to one criterion allowing to compensate loss with respect to another' and not in terms of 'importance' of criteria (even if that attitude is still often encountered).

In a method such as ELECTRE I, the interpretation of the weights is completely different. In this method, the weight of a criterion plays the same part as a number of votes in a voting procedure. Formally, in a non-compensatory method (such as ELECTRE I), one can define a 'more important than' relation on the set of coalitions of criteria. Given two coalitions of criteria G and H (two subsets of family F), 'G is more important than H' if two (real or fictive) actions a and b can be found such that

$$\begin{cases} a \text{ is better than } b \text{ for all criteria in } G, \\ b \text{ is better than } a \text{ for all criteria in } H, \\ a \text{ and } b \text{ are indifferent for all the other criteria,} \\ a \text{ is globally better than } b \end{cases}$$

(because of non-compensation, one can be sure that the latter definition won't lead to any contradiction). If one assumes that this 'more important than' relation can be represented using n constants $p_1, p_2, ..., p_n$ (associated to the n criteria) such that the comparison between G and H is equivalent to that between $\sum_{j \in G} p_j$ and $\sum_{j \in H} p_j$, one is taken back to well-known non-compensatory methods (on this subject, see Vansnick, 1986a). From a theoretical point of view, this allows some necessary and sufficient existence conditions for these 'weights' to be established (see, for example, Doignon and Falmagne, 1991). In practice, their determination can be deduced from comparisons between real or fictive actions.

Another way of characterizing the nature of the weights used in a method consists in seeking the transformations of these weights which are allowed without any modification of the method's results and finding inspiration in the results of meaningfulness theory (cf. Roberts, 1985; Roberts and Rosenbaum, 1986). In a deterministic context, most methods authorize a multiplication of weights by a positive constant (this allows the weights to be normalized by making them sum to 1). In the weighted average method, the latter is the only transformation which is allowed (one says that the 'weights' make up a ratio scale). In the ELECTRE I method, any transformation preserving the order of the coalitions' weights is authorized (the weight of a coalition being the sum of the weights of the criteria composing it). A great deal of research remains to be done in this direction.

From a practical point of view, several methods have been proposed in the literature to estimate the 'weights' of the criteria, without the authors always being interested in their interpretation in function of the use which is made of them. Eckenrode (1966) compares experimentally six methods (ranking by order of importance, valuation of importance on a given scale, different types of pairwise comparisons) in which the decision-maker can immediately conclude on the relative importance of the criteria. More recently, the Saaty method (1980) has been the target of a lot of criticism (see, for example, Belton, 1986). The reader will also find a proposal for a methodology in Vansnick (1986b).

It is remarkable to notice that, very often, the person who is interrogated will spontaneously award weights to the criteria. One can therefore wonder, in order to use them adequately, what they represent in terms of preferences. To our knowledge, very few experiments have been made up to now on this subject (see Drugman, 1990). More generally, research today is mostly being directed toward the understanding and formalization of the concept of importance (Mousseau, 1989; Roy, 1990b).

Finally, in this problem of determination of 'weights', it is clearly utopian to hope for any precision: it is preferable to consider several series of weights or to analyse the feasible weight space (such as in Bana e Costa, 1986, 1988; or Climaco *et al.*, 1987; or the work by Roy, Present and Silhol which will be mentioned in section 13).

2.3 INDEPENDENCE OF CRITERIA

Clearly, the definition of the criteria implies that each one is preferentially independent in F (cf. Chapter 3, section 15). One must indeed be able to speak of preferences according to one criterion without having to refer to the others.

Most methods go further and implicitly assume a hypothesis of the 'preferential independence of any subfamily of criteria' type. This is clearly the case of the additive model in multiple attribute utility theory (Chapter 4, section 2), but it is also the case (even if the condition is weaker) in outranking methods (see Roy and Bouyssou, 1987b, on this subject).

Many people wonder which attitude to take when, in a given problem, two criteria appear to be strongly correlated (in the sense of the correlation coefficients of statistics). The fact that two criteria are strongly correlated is, in general, due to the existence of some factors which influence both criteria in the same direction (a direct functional dependence between the two criteria is excluded if family F of criteria is consistent, because of the non-redundancy condition). Due to the complexity of the links which may occur through these factors, it is utopian to try to redefine family F in a way which avoids any correlation between the criteria (even if this must be avoided as far as possible). Furthermore, eliminating a criterion because it is strongly correlated with another destroys information which, in decision-aid terms, is not necessarily redundant and may therefore be useful, if not indispensable.

3. ARROW'S THEOREM

Let A be a finite set of actions, S_A the set of complete preorders (complete and transitive relations; cf. Chapter 2) on A and S_A^n the set of n-tuples of complete preorders on A. Given a complete preorder S_i on A, we denote by P_i the relation defined by

$$a P_i b \text{ iff } a S_i b \text{ and } b \mathcal{S}_i a.$$

From here on, we call an *aggregation procedure* a function

$$f: S_A^n \longrightarrow S_A.$$

Arrow's theorem can be stated as follows: *if the number of elements of A is larger or equal to 3, no aggregation procedure exists which simultaneously satisfies the following conditions:*

- $\forall \, (S_1,\ldots,S_n)\in S_A^n$, $\forall \, a,b\in A$: aP_ib, $\forall \, i \Rightarrow aSb$ and $b\mathcal{S}a$, where

  $S = f(S_1,\ldots,S_n)$ (*unanimity*);

- $\exists i \in \{1,\ldots,n\}$ such that $\forall \, (S_1,\ldots,S_n)\in S_A^n$, $\forall \, a,b\in A$:

  $aP_ib \Rightarrow aSb$ and $b\mathcal{S}a$, where $S = f(S_1,\ldots,S_n)$ (*non-dictatorship*);

- $\forall \, (S_1,\ldots,S_n)$, $(S_1',\ldots,S_n')\in S_A^n$, $\forall \, a,b\in A$:

if $(S_1,\ldots,S_n)_{/a,b} = (S_1',\ldots,S_n')_{/a,b'}$ if $S = f(S_1,\ldots,S_n)$ and if $S' = f(S_1',\ldots,S_n')$, then $S_{/a,b} = S_{/a,b}'$ where $S_{/a,b}$ denotes the restriction of S to set $\{a,b\}$ and $(S_1,\ldots,S_n)_{/a,b} = (S_{1/a,b},\ldots,S_{n/a,b})$ (*independence of irrelevant alternatives*).

Arrow's theorem is probably one of the results most frequently studied in the literature: it gave birth to numerous variations in which the different conditions are made more or less constraining. Its interpretation has also been the subject of great discussion but can be summarized as follows: the information contained in n complete preorders is not sufficient to univocally determine a complete preorder which aggregates them. Faced with this assertion, two reactions are possible.

(1) some extra information must be added;
(2) one must allow a structure less rich than a global complete preorder.

Both these trends have been followed in the literature.

(1) The independence of irrelevant alternatives forbids any idea of preference intensity and 'intercriterion' comparison. Many authors have shown that the introduction of such concepts makes it possible to find 'rational' aggregation procedures (i.e. satisfying conditions similar to Arrow's). Keeney (1976a), for example, established conditions allowing the aggregation of cardinal utility functions through linear combinations of these utilities. Other authors have considered the case where some information on the relative importance of the complete preorders is at hand. All this work fits in option 1; furthermore, if there is a lot of extra information, it is clear that the result may be even more rich than a simple complete preorder, as can be seen in the work on utility function aggregation by Von Neumann–Morgenstern.
(2) Many authors have studied Arrow's problem statement in the case where the global relation, aggregating the n complete preorders, is less rich than a complete preorder: partial order, quasi-transitive relation,

relation with no circuit, tournament, etc. In some cases, the impossibility theorem becomes a possibility theorem.

It may also happen that the n relations to be aggregated are not complete preorders, but less rich structures. Some authors have studied Arrow's problem statement in that context, with a global relation which is also a less rich structure than a complete preorder. Others have searched for complete preorders closest to the n given relations, for different distances.

Anyone interested by all these results will find all relevant information in the following references: Arrow (1951), Aumann (1969), Batra and Pattanaik (1972), Blau (1972), Fishburn (1970c, 1970d, 1974b), Keeney (1976), Kreweras (1976), Monjardet (1973, 1978a), Osborne (1976), Sen (1977) and Vincke (1982b, 1982c).

Let us also mention the interesting book by Arrow and Raynaud (1986), in which a new system of axioms is proposed, along with some aggregation techniques for complete preorders which are compatible with these axioms.

Arrow's impossibility theorem doesn't mean that multicriteria decision-aid is vain: the context in which multicriteria problems are set is often very far from the theoretical frame given by Arrow (cf. Roy and Bouyssou, 1987c). Nevertheless, the work described above brings an enlightenment which shouldn't be ignored by multicriteria problem specialists.

4. VOTING PROCEDURES

We consider the problem of a jury which must select one person from a set of candidates. Two fundamental questions have been considered in the literature about this particular problem: we will illustrate them through examples.

Let $A = \{a,b,c\}$ and consider a jury of 9 persons who have the following preferences:

$$aPbPc \text{ for three members,}$$

$$bPcPa \text{ for two members,}$$

$$cPaPb \text{ for one member,}$$

$$aPcPb \text{ for one member,}$$

$$cPbPa \text{ for two members.}$$

The voting procedure adopted by this jury is the following (Lhuilier's procedure): a candidate is elected if he is the best for more than half of the voters; if no candidate satisfies the latter condition, the candidate who is ranked first or second by most voters is chosen. In the example given above, b is elected.

One must note, however, that this procedure leads to a result which is in contradiction with pairwise comparisons of the candidates since five voters out of nine prefer a to b. In fact, this type of situation may occur in any voting procedure. On the other hand, it is well known that the method of pairwise comparisons may lead to circuits and thus doesn't yield any solution to the problem (in our example, it yields aPbPcPa).

The first fundamental question thus lies in the impossibility of finding a voting procedure which always yields a solution and which never contradicts pairwise comparisons. One possible solution is to seek a procedure which, in a way, minimizes the number of contradictions with respect to pairwise comparisons or maximizes the probability of avoiding these contradictions.

Now consider a jury of three voters who must give their opinion about set $A = \{a,b,c,d\}$. The voters' preferences are the following:

$$a\text{P}b\text{P}c\text{P}d \text{ for voter I,}$$

$$d\text{P}a\text{P}b\text{P}c \text{ for voter II,}$$

$$d\text{P}a\text{P}b\text{P}c \text{ for voter III.}$$

The procedure chosen here consists in awarding four points to a candidate ranked first by a voter, three points if he is second, and so forth, and to elect the candidate having obtained the highest score. In our example, a is elected with a total of 10 points.

Now assume that voter III wishes to favour d and that he knows that a is a dangerous opponent. He can then declare that his preference ordering is

$$d\text{P}b\text{P}c\text{P}a,$$

thereby succeeding in getting d elected. This example illustrates the fundamental problem of voting procedures being 'manipulated' (i.e. the possibility left to a member of the jury to vote in function of the voting procedure which is chosen and not of his preferences). The most important result in this frame is that of Gibbard (1973), proving the impossibility of finding a voting procedure which is simultaneously non-dictatorial and non-manipulable.

Anyone interested by voting procedures can find extra information in Batteau and Blin (1976), Fishburn (1971), Gibbard (1973), Monjardet (1976), Peleg (1978) and Vincke (1982c). The link with multicriteria methods is perfectly illustrated in Vansnick (1986a) (see also sections 1.3 and 1.4 of this chapter).

5. CHOICE FUNCTIONS

A choice function is a function C which associates, to each subset B of A, a subset $C(B)$ of B. Given a preference structure on A, it can be associated with a choice function, such as, for example

$$C(B) = \{a \in B : aPb \text{ or } aIb, \ \forall \ b \in B\}$$

or

$$C(B) = \{a \in B : \not\exists \ b \in B : bPa\}.$$

Many results have been established concerning the links between properties of preference structures and those of the choice functions which are associated with them. In particular, Arrow's theorem (cf. section 3) can be reformulated in terms of choice functions.

The study of these functions is particularly interesting in the frame of choice problem statements; it allows a better understanding of the properties which are inherent to some widely used selection procedures (majority rule, non-minority rule, etc.).

Anyone interested can find extra information mainly in the following references: Brown (1975), Fishburn (1975, 1976b, 1977), Herzberger (1973), Jamison and Lau (1973), Pattanaik (1970), Plott (1973), Sen (1977) and Vincke (1982c).

6. MULTIPLE OBJECTIVE MATHEMATICAL PROGRAMMING

Multiple objective mathematical programs (cf. Chapter 3, section 3) make up the most frequently studied class of multicriteria problems in the literature (see, for example, Buchanan, 1986; Steuer, 1986; Narula and Weistroffer, 1989; Rios Insua, 1990; Vanderpooten, 1990a). This can be easily explained by the diversity of assumptions which can be made on the variables (continuous, integer, boolean, etc.) as well as on functions

h_i and g_j (linearity, convexity, differentiability, etc.), and by the important theoretical frame which is already at hand in mathematical programming.

The subject most frequently studied undoubtedly concerns the set of efficient actions (or solutions) (cf. Chapter 3, section 8). Their characterization and their properties have been studied by many authors, mostly in the linear case (Ecker *et al.*, 1980; Evans and Steuer, 1973; Gal, 1977; Philip, 1972; Yu and Zeleny, 1975). In particular, the following problems have been examined:

- how to check if a solution is efficient;
- how to obtain all efficient vertices;
- what are the links between the set of efficient solutions, the set of points closest to the ideal point (for different distances) and the set of solutions which optimize functions aggregating the *n* criteria (see Chapter 3, section 14 for some theorems of this type in the general case of multicriteria problems);
- how does the set of efficient solutions vary with respect to different perturbations brought on to the data (adding or eliminating criteria, variations in the constraints or the criteria);
- how to reduce the set of efficient solutions.

Some variants on the concept of efficiency have also been proposed (Geoffrion, 1968; Lowe *et al.*, 1984) in order to simplify the procedures.

Another theoretical subject concerns the generalization, to the multiobjective case, of the concept of duality: some examples of the latter can be found in Ignizio (1984), Isermann (1978) and Rodder (1977).

Concerning the methods, it is interesting to note how researchers' preoccupations have evolved: they were at first only interested in finding efficient solutions, then, little by little, they turned to the interactive search for a compromise solution; several among the interactive procedures described in Chapter 6 were first developed in the frame of multiple objective mathematical programming. This evolution clearly illustrates the transition from what was called MCDM (multicriteria decision-making) to what is more and more often called MCDA (multicriteria decision-aid).

A special word must be said for the methodology of 'goal programming' which, by itself, is the centre of numerous theoretical and applied studies. This methodology rests on the following basic scheme:

(1) set the values one wishes to attain on each criterion (these are the objectives);

(2) assign priorities (weights) to these objectives;
(3) define (positive or negative) deviations with respect to these objectives;
(4) minimize the weighted sum of these deviations;
(5) perform a sensitivity analysis.

   This methodology, first developed in the frame of linear programming, was extended to all other types of mathematical programs and was also rendered interactive. Anyone interested will find extra information in Charnes and Cooper (1977), Spronk (1981), Steuer (1986) and Romero (1986).
   A remarkable book by Steuer (1986) is devoted to multiple objective mathematical programming; we summarize it in our bibliography. In particular, the book gives references on subjects such as bicriterion mathematical programming, duality, fuzzy multiple objective programming (also summarized by Teghem and Kunsch, 1986b), multiple objective game theory, multiple objective dynamic programming and multiple objective statistics.
   Finally, up to now, relatively little research has been devoted to multiple objective stochastic programming: let us mention the work of Goicoechea *et al.* (1982), Leclercq (1982), Stancu-Minasian (1984, 1990), Teghem *et al.* (1986a), Slowinski and Teghem (1990).

7. MULTICRITERIA PROBLEMS IN GRAPHS

Some classical applications of graph theory were the object of generalizations to the multicriteria case: localization problems (Chalmet *et al.*, 1981; Lowe, 1978; Vincke, 1983), shortest path problems (Cox *et al.*, 1980; Martins, 1984; Vincke, 1984), scheduling problems (Huckert *et al.*, 1980; Slowinski, 1981; Van Wassenhove and Gelders, 1980).

8. TAKING RISK INTO ACCOUNT

The consideration of risk in decision-making and the modelling of the decision-maker's attitude when confronted with risk were mostly examined in the context of multiple attribute utility theory. Nevertheless, attitude when confronted with risk often results from several aspects requiring a multicriteria treatment. For a summary of these problems along with a thorough bibliography, see Colson (1985).

9. FUZZY SETS AND MULTICRITERIA DECISION-AID

In order to take into account the unavoidable lack of precision, ambiguity, and nuances which appear in decision-making problems, it is quite natural to turn to fields such as the theory of fuzzy sets. An abundant literature has been published on the subject as much on problems of modelling and aggregation of preferences (Kacprzyk and Roubens, 1988; Leberling, 1981; Orlovsky, 1978; Roubens and Vincke, 1983a, 1987, 1988; Barrett *et al.*, 1990) as on multiple objective mathematical programming problems (Slowinski, 1986; Zimmermann, 1978, 1986; Zimmermann, 1984; Sakawa and Yano, 1990).

10. NEGOTIATION-AID

For several years, some authors have been interested in the conception of scientific methods for negotiation-aid. The aim is to find some compromise in a decision problem in which are involved several decision-makers (or committees) with different systems of preferences (while, in multicriteria decision-aid, the decision-maker is unique, even if it is a committee). As examples, let us mention the work of Jacquet-Lagrèze (1981), Kersten (1985), Kersten and Szapiro (1986), Kersten and Szpakowicz (1990), Wendel (1980), Shakun (1987). We also recommend to any interested reader, the special edition of the *European Journal of Operational Research* (**46**(2), 1990) devoted to this subject.

11. MULTICRITERIA DECISION-AID SOFTWARE

Drawing up a list of all the software available on the market is quite an arduous task, for at least two reasons. The first is that in addition to the software which is presented as 'commercial products' (by the authors of these products, but not yet by software companies), many high-quality computer programs exist in universities but only researchers are able to use them: all the methods presented in this book have been programmed many times, more or less well, and, depending upon the need, in different research laboratories: it is impossible today to give an inventory of these programs. The second reason is the rapidity of development of this software which renders irrelevant any attempt at comment or comparison.

   It is therefore too early to draw up a conclusion and recommend a library of software to the future user. Bearing in mind the latter and with the absolute certainty of being incomplete, let us mention the following software: PREFCALC (Jacquet-Lagrèze, 1984a), ELECTRE IS (Roy and Skalka, 1984a), ELECTRE III and IV (Skalka *et al.*, 1984), PROMCALC and GAIA (Mareschal, 1988a,b), ORESTE (Pastijn *et al.*, 1988), GPSTEM (Fichefet, 1976), VIG (Korhonen, 1987), TRIMAP (Climaco *et al.*, 1987), NEGO (Kersten, 1985), MAPPAC/PRAGMA (Matarazzo, 1986, 1988), TRICHOM (Moscarola and Roy, 1977) IMGP (Spronk, 1981), VISA (Belton, 1990), STRANGE (Teghem *et al.*, 1986a), EXPERT CHOICE (Saaty, 1980), PRIAM (Levine and Pomerol, 1986) and MARS (Colson, 1989).

We also recommend the list given by Despontin *et al.* (1983) which is currently being updated. Finally, concerning software which is more specifically linked to multiple objective mathematical programming, the reader is referred to Steuer (1986).

12. EXPERT SYSTEMS AND MULTICRITERIA DECISION-AID

The current development of artificial intelligence and its proximity to operations research couldn't leave specialists of multicriteria decision-aid indifferent. Although very few papers have been published up to now, there are more and more related working papers and conferences.

As an example, let us mention the PRIAM method (Levine and Pomerol, 1986), an interactive program involving a heuristic exploration of the set of actions, through reasoning inspired by that of artificial intelligence; this method has also been adapted to multiple objective linear programming (Pomerol and Trabelsi, 1987). We also mention the work of Jacquet-Lagrèze and Shakun (1984b).

13. APPLICATIONS OF MULTICRITERIA DECISION-AID

It is impossible in the frame of this book to give a detailed description of the characteristic applications of multicriteria decision-aid. In any case, it is remarkable to notice that the formulation of decision problems in multicriteria terms is becoming more and more frequent in fields which are as different as production, marketing, economy, safety, environment, finance, engineering, energy, transport, and so on. We give here under a (non-exhaustive, of course) list of references involving real-life problems. One should add to the list the many related university dissertations.

In the general bibliography given at the end of the book, the following references also include some applications: Bana e Costa (1988), Buffet *et al.* (1967), Despontin and Vincke (1977), Fandel and Spronk (1985), Geoffrion *et al.* (1972), Goicoechea *et al.* (1982), Hwang and Masud (1979), Jacquet-Lagrèze and Siskos (1983), Moscarola and Roy (1977), Roy and Bertier (1973), Hugonnard and Roy (1982), Roy (1985), Steuer (1986). Also, the bibliography of Siskos *et al.* (1983) contains quite a long list of applications of outranking methods.

The following references, more specifically devoted to a particular real-life problem, are not included in the general bibliography.

Abgueguen R. (1971) *La sélection des supports de presse.* R. Laffont, Paris.

Barda O., Dupuis J. and Lencioni P. (1990) Multicriteria location of thermal power plants, *European Journal of Operational Research*, **45**, 332–346.

Bertier P. and de Montgolfier J. (1974) On multicriteria analysis: an application to a forest management problem, *Metra*, **III**(1), 33–45.

Briggs T., Kunsch, P. and Mareschal, B. (1990) Nuclear waste management: an application of the multicriteria Promethee methods, *European Journal of Operational Research*, **44**, 1–10.

Camier L., Martin, M. and Raimbault M. (1974) Modèle de décision en présence de critères multiples: choix d'investissement en matière d'équipement hydraulique, AFCET Congress, Vol. I, Paris.

Casteignau M., Guy M. and Roy B. (1991) L'analyse multicritère interactive comme outil d'aide à la décision pour la gestion des risques environnementaux et industriels. Proceedings of the international congress 'Innovations, progrès industriels et environnementaux', Strasbourg.

Dubois P., Brans, J. P., Cantraine, F. and Mareschal, B. (1989) MEDICIS: an expert system for computer-aided diagnosis using the Promethee multicriteria method, *European Journal of Operational Research*, **39**(3), 284–292.

Despontin M. (1982) Regional multiple objective quantitative economic policy: a Belgian model, *European Journal of Operational Research*, **10**(1), 82–89.

Grassin N. (1986) Constructing criteria for the comparison of different options of high voltage line route, *Cahier du Lamsade*, 69, Université Paris-Dauphine (see also *European Journal of Operational Research*, **26**(1), 42–58).

Hallefjord A., Jornsten K. and Eriksson O. (1986) A long range forestry planning problem with multiple objectives, *European Journal of Operational Research*, **26**(1), 123–133.

Hugonnard J. and Roy B. (1983) Le plan d'extension du métro en banlieue parisienne, in *Méthode de décision multicritère*, E. Jacquet-Lagrèze and J. Siskos (eds.), Editions Hommes et Techniques, 39–66.

Kunsch P. and Teghem J. (1987) Nuclear fuel cycle optimization using multiobjective stochastic linear programming, *European Journal of Operational Research*, **31**, 240–249.

Lemaire J., Reinhard J. M. and Vincke Ph. (1981) A new approach to reinsurance: multicriteria analysis, in *Net Retensions*, NRG Publications, Amsterdam.

Lootsma F., Meisner J. and Schellemans F. (1986) (Multicriteria decision analysis as an aid to the strategic planning of energy R & D, *European Journal of Operational Research*, **25**, 216–234.

Loucks D. (1977) An application of interactive multiobjective water resources planning, *Interfaces*, **8**(1), 70–75.

Martel J. M. and D'Avignon G. (1982) Projects ordering with multicriteria analysis, *European Journal of Operational Research*, **10**(1), 56–69.

Massam B. (1981) The search for the best route: an application of a formal method using multiple criteria, *Cahier du Lamsade*, 37, Université Paris-Dauphine.

Moscarola J. (1978) Multicriteria decision aid: two applications in education management, in *Multiple Criteria Problem Solving*, S. Zionts (ed.), Springer Verlag, n° 155.

Norese M. F. and Ostanello A. (1985) A multicriteria model for an evaluation of supply/demand of sport facilities in a metropolitan area, *Airo*, 1985, 467–492.

Ostanello A. and Norese, M. F. (1978) Multicriteria analysis of industrial localisation: experimentation on the territorial zones of Turin area, *Airo*, 1978, 393–411.

Renard F. (1986) Utilisation d'ELECTRE dans l'analyse des réponses à un appel d'offres: le cas de la machine de tri paquets à la Direction Générale des Postes, *Cahier du Lamsade*, 73, Université Paris-Dauphine.

Roba E., Sussmann B. and Theys M. (1970) Les méthodes de choix multicritères appliquées à la sélection du personnel, in *Models of Manpower Systems*, A. Smith (ed.), English University Press, Paris.

Rohmer J. and Veret J. (1980) Choix d'une stratégie commerciale dans la distribution succursaliste en présence de critères multiples, *Cahier du Lamsade*, 31, Université Paris-Dauphine.

Romero C. and Rehman T. (1989) *Multiple Criteria Analysis for Agricultural Decisions*, Elsevier.

Roy B. and Bouyssou D. (1986) Comparison of two decision-aid models applied to a nuclear plan siting example, *European Journal of Operational Research*, **25**, 200–215.

Roy B., Present M. and Silhol D. (1983) Programmation de la rénovation des stations du métro parisien: un cas d'application de la méthode ELECTRE III, *Document du Lamsade*, 24, Université Paris-Dauphine (see also *European Journal of Operational Research*, **24**(1), 318–334, 1986).

Roy B., Letellier, F. and Hougas, B. (1990) Un modèle multicritère de réapprovisionnement sur deux niveaux de stockage, *Revue Générale des Chemins de Fer*, **109**, 37–40.

Roy B., Slowinski, R. and Treichel, W. (1991) Multicriteria programming of rural water supply systems, *Document du Lamsade*, 65, Université Paris-Dauphine.

Saurais O. and Siskos J. (1980) L'approche multicritère: application au lancement d'un nouveau jeu de plage, *Méthodologie de la recherche en marketing*, FNEGE, Lille, 341–389.

Schnabele P. and Parent E. (1988) Le choix d'un aménagement aquacole, *Document du Lamsade*, 47, Université Paris-Dauphine.

Simos J. (1990) *Evaluer l'impact sur l'environnement: une approche originale par l'analyse multicritère et la négociation*, Presses polytechniques et universitaires romandes.

Siskos J., Lombard J. and Oudiz A. (1985) The use of outranking methods in the comparison of control options against a chemical pollutant, *Cahier du Lamsade*, 58, Université Paris-Dauphine.

Siskos J. (1982) Evaluating a system of furniture retail outlets using an interactive ordinal regression method, *Cahier du Lamsade*, 38, Université Paris-Dauphine.

Slowinski R. (1981) Problèmes d'allocation de moyens limités en présence de critère multiples, *Cahier du Lamsade*, 36, Université Paris-Dauphine.

Zopounidis C. (1985) Evaluation multicritère du risque de faillite d'entreprises: méthodologie et application, *Cahier du Lamsade*, 66, Université Paris-Dauphine.

14. SOME ROUTES FOR FURTHER RESEARCH

As mentioned earlier, it rarely happens that the actions and criteria of a decision problem are objective realities which are easy to grasp and model. Multicriteria decision-aid implies that the scientist, before attempting to apply a method, should help the decision-maker to define these elements, and the latter may be one of his most arduous tasks. Little research has been developed on this problem. To our best knowledge, only Roy (1985) has proposed a methodology to deal with that question: his work should be the starting point of many experiments and research projects.

In the same direction, the decision-maker's preferences are often assumed to exist a priori. It may happen, however, that the decision-maker doesn't have any information at hand allowing him to express his preferences clearly. In such a case, the scientist's role is to help the decision-maker to discover them and make them explicit. Some research on the manner in which a person should be interrogated and his preferences represented in an operational way would be quite useful. This field is already studied, mainly in the USA, by 'psychologist-mathematicians', but very little work has been done in the multicriteria context.

The two previous aspects illustrate quite well the fact that solving a multicriteria problem represents much more than a simple aggregation of 'given' preferences on a 'given' set.

The preference structures defined in Chapter 2 and including the concepts of thresholds are relatively recent and haven't yet been systematically introduced in multicriteria decision-aid (we have only encountered them in some outranking methods; see Chapter 5). One research direction thus consists in generalizing the theoretical results and the methods by including those structures; in particular, the following problems should be considered:

- how to define the dominance relation and the efficient actions in the presence of thresholds;
- how to define substitution rates;
- how to define preferential independence;
- how to generalize multiple attribute utility theory and the resulting methods;
- how to introduce thresholds in interactive procedures.

Furthermore, as was shown in section 1, the introduction of thresholds in 'elementary' methods such as the weighted average or the lexicographic method brings on many new problems.

As for intercriterion information, the most difficult problem remains that of the modelling of the relative importance of the criteria (see section 2).

Many decision problems include random variables translating the uncertainty of the data. Dealing with these elements through multiple attribute utility theory is well established (Von Neumann and Morgenstern, 1967; Fishburn, 1970a, 1982; Keeney and Raiffa, 1976b), but such is not the case for the other approaches (except for the work mentioned in Chapter 5, section 10 and at the end of section 6 of this chapter).

More generally, each of the three important approaches presented in Chapters 4, 5 and 6 presents gaps which should be filled:

- for multiple attribute utility theory, extension to situations involving less restrictive assumptions;
- for outranking methods, a basic theory;
- for interactive procedures, good software and real-life applications.

Finally, we feel that bringing together multicriteria decision-aid and artificial intelligence could only help to deal with decision problems more realistically (cf. Simon, 1987).

15. TOWARDS A MULTICRITERIA DECISION-AID THEORY

The choice of a multicriteria method is often made on the basis of relatively subjective arguments (past experience, existence of suitable software, etc.). We believe that it is possible to develop a theory that would allow that choice to be made more rigorously. For this, it is necessary to know the assumptions which are implicitly included in the methods, i.e. to arrive at a characterization of each of them through properties which can be intuitively interpreted. This is the perspective in which can be placed the recent work of Bouyssou (1990), Bouyssou and Perny (1990) and Vincke (1991).

Bibliography

1. INTRODUCTION

Let us first recall that, in Chapter 7, section 13, we gave a list of references more specifically devoted to applications of multicriteria decision-aid. In this chapter, we give:

- in section 2: a description of the books by A. Scharlig (1985), B. Roy (1985) and R. Steuer (1986);
- in section 3: a list of references following the alphabetical order of authors and chronological order for each author; for each reference, we indicate the chapter(s) and section(s) to which it refers more specifically;
- in section 4: the reference numbers ordered by chapter;
- in section 5: a list of keywords.

Some journals have devoted special issues to multicriteria decision-aid, such as, for example: *Management Science*, **30**(11) (1984); *European Journal of Operational Research*, **25**(2) (1986), **26**(1) (1986) and **46**(2) (1990); *Mathematical and Computer Modelling*, **12**(10) (1989).

Let us also note the existence of the *Cahiers* and *Documents du Lamsade* (Université Paris-Dauphine), mainly devoted to multicriteria decision-aid.

Finally, we give below the list of the volumes which are relative to preference modelling and multicriteria analysis, in the Springer-Verlag series Lecture Notes in Economics and Mathematical Systems.

Vol. 95 (1974): Zeleny, M., *Linear multiobjective programming*.
Vol. 112 (1975): Wilhelm, J., *Objectives and multi-objective decision-making under uncertainty*.
Vol. 123 (1976): Zeleny, M. (ed), *Multiple criteria decision making*.
Vol. 130 (1976): Thiriez, H. and Zionts, S. (eds), *Multiple criteria decision making*.
Vol. 155 (1978): Zionts, S. (ed), *Multiple criteria problem solving*.

Vol. 164 (1979): Hwang, C. and Masud, A., *Multiple objective decision making: methods and applications.*
Vol. 177 (1980): Fandel, G. and Gal, T. (eds), *Multiple criteria decision making: theory and application.*
Vol. 186 (1981): Hwang, C. and Yoon, K., *Multiple attribute decision making: methods and applications.*
Vol. 190 (1981): Morse, J. (ed), *Organizations: multiple agents with multiple criteria.*
Vol. 209 (1983): Hansen, P. (ed), *Essays and surveys on multiple criteria decision making.*
Vol. 229 (1984): Grauer, M. and Wierzbicki, A. (eds), *Interactive decision analysis.*
Vol. 230 (1984): Despontin, M., Nijkamp P. and Spronk, J. (eds), *Macro-economic planning with conflicting goals.*
Vol. 242 (1985): Haimes, Y. and Chankong, V. (eds), *Decision making with multiple objectives.*
Vol. 250 (1985): Roubens, M. and Vincke, Ph., *Preference modelling.*
Vol. 273 (1986): Fandel, G., Grauer, M., Kurzhanski, A. and Wierzbicki, A. (eds), *Large scale modelling and interactive decision analysis.*
Vol. 281 (1987): Hwang, C. and Lin, M., *Group decision making under multiple criteria.*
Vol. 301 (1988): Kacprzyk, J. and Roubens, M. (ed), *Non-conventional preference relations in decision making.*
Vol. 319 (1989): Dinh The Luc, *Theory of vector optimization.*
Vol. 347 (1990): Rios Insua, D., *Sensitivity analysis in multiobjective decision making.*

2. DESCRIPTION OF THREE BOOKS

(1) *Décider sur plusieurs critères*

Alain Schärlig, Presses Polytechniques Romandes, ISBN 2-88074-073-8, 1985.

This book by Alain Schärlig was the first to give a complete outline of the different approaches which have been proposed up to now in multicriteria analysis, including methods from the American as well as the French school.

After criticizing, in chapter 1, the traditional approach of optimization through its postulates and bad experiences, in chapter 2, Alain Schärlig explains the reasons for which decision problems are often multicriteria and the cultural phenomena which, for a long time, kept the idea from being further developed.

Chapter 3 describes the three first steps of a decision-aid procedure: defining the potential actions, enumerating the criteria, evaluating each action according to each criterion. Thereafter follows the presentation of the fourth step, i.e. aggregation, and of the three fundamental attitudes which are encountered: complete transitive aggregation (see our Chapter 4), partial aggregation (see our Chapter 5) and local iterative aggregation (see our Chapter 6). The remainder of the book is devoted to the description of methods and applications pertaining to these different attitudes.

Chapter 4 concerns complete aggregation methods: the weighted average, the product of ratios, 'les déclassements comparés', the hierarchic method, multiple attribute utility theory and the UTA method. Some important applications are described in chapter 5.

Two delicate problems closely linked to multicriteria analysis are examined in chapters 6 and 7: in education, the treatment of student grades and voting procedures. The author illustrates all the traps pertaining to these problems.

In chapter 8, partial aggregation methods are examined, i.e. methods which have been developed during the last twenty years by the French school, of which the author is undoubtedly a member: the ELECTRE methods and their variations, trichotomic procedures, PROMETHEE, QUALIFLEX and ORESTE are presented briefly and illustrated in chapter 9 using real-life applications.

Iterative local aggregation is examined in chapters 10 and 11, where the reader will find, in particular, the evolving target procedure, improvement cones, the methods of Zionts and Wallenius, Geoffrion and Dyer, Benayoun and Tergny, interactive goal programming and some applications.

As Alain Schärlig rightly says, the book, which requires no prior knowledge, is above all aimed at 'creating a desire': the reader won't find any detailed user's guide or mathematical justifications of the methods described; to that end, the reader is referred to the references carefully mentioned by the author. On the other hand, he will find in this book a good description of the multicriterion viewpoint, i.e. 'putting an individual at the centre of the problem, with mathematics around him as peripheral instruments, rather than putting mathematics in the centre and reducing the individual to what they are capable of understanding of him'. Alain Schärlig must be given credit for having perfectly illustrated the latter point of view while using a very personal style, rendering his book quite pleasant to read.

This book should play quite an important part in easing contacts between 'scientists' (researchers) and 'decision-makers' (practitioners): indeed, the former have a basic reference to propose in order to introduce the others into the ever expanding field of multicriteria analysis.

(2) *Méthodologie multicritére d'aide à la décision*

Bernard Roy, Economica, ISBN 2-7178-0901-5, 1985.

Bernard Roy's book is not simply an enumeration of multicriteria methods; in fact, he proposes a complete methodology for decision-aid. The author gives a detailed description of the preliminary questions associated with any decision problem and the difficulties which are met when choosing a model, as well as of the modelling and aggregation of preferences. Let us also note that a second volume is currently in preparation and will be more specifically devoted to the description and analysis of particular multicriteria methods.

The introductory part of the book examines some questions which are too often left aside in the literature on decision theory: how is a decision made? who are the actors? what is a decision-aid model? In chapters 1 and 2, the author proposes some answers to these questions, based upon his long experience in the field. Chapter 3 presents 12 real-life problems which are to be used further on in the book to illustrate the different concepts which are introduced. Chapter 4 gives some preliminary definitions and describes the principles of the proposed general methodology.

The first part of the book (made up by chapters 5 and 6) then presents the different ways which exist to define the set of actions in a decision problem and the different problem statements (choice, sorting, ranking, description) which may be chosen. A large number of examples give a real-life foundation to the definitions which are introduced.

The second part of the book (chapters 7 to 9) is devoted to preference modelling. Roy gives a detailed presentation of the 'fundamental situations of preferences' and the main structures which are used. Modelling of the consequence of actions is explained in chapter 8, in particular the question of taking into account the unavoidable imprecision, uncertainty and indetermination phenomena. Chapter 9 introduces the concept of criterion, which is the basis for comparisons between actions: the delicate passage from the model of consequences of actions to the construction of criteria is given a detailed analysis, leading to the definition of different types of criteria. The whole second part also emphasizes the dangers of modelling too rapidly.

The third part (chapters 10 to 12) examines aggregation of criteria. After defining the concept of consistent family of criteria and analysing the problem of dependence, Roy comments on the three classical approaches to multicriteria decision-aid: aggregation into a unique criterion (see our Chapter 4), outranking relations (see our Chapter 5) and the interactive approach (see our Chapter 6). A final chapter examines special problems such as choosing an approach, the problem of dependence between actions, and problems with multiple scenarios.

As we noted earlier, the author insists much more on the methodology than on the techniques (to which the second volume will be devoted), the admitted goal being to set the foundations for a 'science of decision-aid'. This is why great importance is awarded to the vocabulary (a basis of communication, but also a tool of reflection).

Roy's book summarizes quite rigorously the different aspects of decision-aid and, for the first time, proposes a coherent methodology. It is an indispensable tool for anyone wishing to study this field thoroughly.

To end, let us mention that this book can be read at three different levels (indicated in the margin): an introduction to multicriteria decision-aid for beginners, a study of important questions for persons with some knowledge, and an analysis of the details and open problems for specialists.

(3) *Multiple criteria optimization: theory, computation and application*

Ralph Steuer, John Wiley and Sons, ISBN 0-471-88846-X, 1986.

In his introduction, Ralph Steuer divides multicriteria decision problems into two categories: on the one hand, problems which are characterized by a small number of solutions and an uncertain environment; on the other, deterministic problems which encompass a great number of solutions. According to him, the former are dependent on 'multiattribute analysis' (which we call multiple attribute utility theory) and the latter on 'multicriterion optimization' (which we call multiple objective mathematical programming). His book is devoted to the second category and essentially concerns the linear case. This classification doesn't appear to us to be quite appropriate since it puts on the same level a way to approach multicriteria problems (multiple attribute utility theory) and a particular category of problems (multiple objective mathematical programs). From our viewpoint, multiple objective mathematical programs can be approached through the theory of multiple attribute utility; on the other hand, the interactive approach does not fit into mathematical programming, even if it was often illustrated in such a context. Finally, this classification leaves no room for outranking methods, which make up another important approach to multicriteria problems.

With the exception of the above-mentioned reservations, Steuer's book is undoubtedly the best existing reference on multiple objective linear programming.

The five first chapters recall the basic concepts of linear programming: linear algebra, the simplex method, duality, post-optimal analysis, parametric programming.

Chapter 6 introduces the concepts of utility function, dominance, efficiency and gives some characterizations of efficient solutions.

In chapters 7 and 8, the author goes into the questions which arise when one wishes to aggregate objective functions by using a linear combination of these functions, in particular the interpretation and determination of the coefficients involved in the linear combination.

Chapter 9 is devoted to what is currently called the 'vector maximum problem', i.e. the determination of the set of efficient solutions to a multiple objective linear program; a computer program is also presented.

The goal programming method makes up chapter 10: the author distinguishes between the archimedian case (objectives are aggregated through a linear combination) and the lexicographic case (objectives are ranked following some priorities).

Chapter 11 describes a certain number of 'filtering' procedures (selection of a sample in a finite but large set) and of 'discretization' (characterization of a continuous set of points through a finite sample), along with the associated computer programs. These procedures are at the heart of the method described in chapter 14.

Chapter 12, which is relatively short, presents an outline of multiple objective fractional programming.

In chapter 13, the author describes some interactive procedures, still in the context of multiple objective programming: therein can be found the methods described in sections 2, 3, 5 and 9 of our Chapter 6, along with the premises of the method of Steuer and Choo (Chapter 6, section 8). The latter, due to the author and based upon a weighted distance of Tchebycheff, is detailed in chapters 14 (basic theory and algorithms) and 15 (computer aspects).

Finally, chapter 16 presents some applications and chapter 17 proposes routes for further research and references on subjects which are close to the theme of the book.

Let us also note that each chapter contains many graphs, examples and exercises which are quite useful for those who teach this subject.

3. REFERENCES

References are given following the alphabetical order of first authors and for each author, following chronological order. The numbers following each reference in square brackets recall the chapter(s) (1,2,. . .) and section(s) (§1,§2, . . .) to which each item refers more particularly.

[1]   Allais, M. (1953) Le comportement de l'homme rationnel devant le risque: critique des postulats et axiomes de l'Ecole Américaine. *Econometrica* **21**, 503–546. **[2§14]**

[2]   Arrow, K. (1951) *Social choice and individual values*. Wiley, New York, 1st edn 1951, 2nd edn 1963. **[7§3]**

[3]   Arrow, K. and Raynaud, H. (1986) *Social choice and multicriterion decision-making*. MIT Press, Cambridge, Mass. **[7§3]**

[4]   Aumann, J. (1969) Measurable utility and the measurable choice theorem. In *La Décision*. Editions du C.N.R.S. **[7§3]**

[5]   Bana e Costa, C. (1986) A multicriteria decision aid methodology to deal with conflicting situations on the weights. *European Journal of Operational Research* **26**(1), 22–34. **[7§2]**

[6]   Bana e Costa, C. (1988) A methodology for sensitivity analysis in three-criteria problems: a case study in municipal management. *European Journal of Operational Research* **33**(2), 159–173. **[7§2,13]**

[7]   Bana e Costa, C. (ed.) (1990) *Readings in multiple criteria decision aid*. Springer-Verlag. **[3,4,5,6]**

[8]   Barrett, C., Pattanaik, P. and Salles, M. (1990) On choosing rationally when preferences are fuzzy. *Fuzzy Sets and Systems* **34**, 197–212. **[7§9]**

[9]   Barthelemy, J. P. and Monjardet, B. (1981) The median procedure in cluster analysis and social science theory. *Mathematical Social Sciences* **1**, 235–267. **[7§1]**

[10] Batra, R. and Pattanaik, P. (1972) Transitive multi-stage majority decision with quasi-transitive individual preferences. *Econometrica* **40**, 1121–1135. **[7§3]**

[11] Batteau, P. and Blin, J. (1976) Sur le problème des procédures de scrutin garantissant une expression sincère des opinions. *Mathématiques et Sciences Humaines* **34**, 45–60. **[7§4]**

[12] Batteau, P., Jacquet-Lagrèze, E. and Monjardet, B. (1981) *Analyse et agrégation des préférences dans les sciences sociales, économiques et de gestion*. Economica. **[2;7§3,4;7§5]**

[13] Bell, D., Keeney, R. and Raiffa, H. (eds) (1977) *Conflicting objectives in decision*. IIASA, Laxenburg and Wiley. **[4,6]**

[14] Belton, V. (1986) A comparison of the analytic hierarchy process and a simple multiattribute value function. *European Journal of Operational Research* **26**(1), 7–21. **[7§2]**

[15] Belton, V. (1990) Visual interactive sensitivity analysis for MCDA. In *Readings in MCDA*, Bana e Costa (ed), Springer-Verlag. **[7§11]**

[16] Benayoun, R. De Montgolfier, J., Tergny, J. and Larichev, O. (1971) Linear programming with multiple objective functions: STEP Method (STEM). *Mathematical Programming* **1**, 366–375. **[6§2]**

[17] Bernard, G. and Besson, M. (1971) Douze méthodes d'analyse multicritère. *Revue Française d'Informatique et de Recherche Opérationnelle* **3**, 19–64. **[7§1]**

[18] Blau, J. (1972) A direct proof of Arrow's theorem. *Econometrica* **40**, 61–67. **[7§3]**

[19] Bouyssou, D. (1984a) Approches descriptives et constructives d'aide à la décision: fondements et comparaison. Thèse, Université Paris-Dauphine. **[7§2]**

[20] Bouyssou, D. (1984b) Decision-aid and utility theory: a critical survey. In *Progress in Utility and Risk Theory*, Hagen, O. and Wenstop, F. (eds), D. Reidel, 181–216. **[2§14]**

[21] Bouyssou, D. and Vansnick, J. C. (1986) Noncompensatory and generalized noncompensatory preference structures. *Theory and Decision* **21**, 251–266. **[7§2]**

[22] Bouyssou, D. (1986) Some remarks on the notion of compensation in MCDM. *European Journal of Operational Research* **26**(1), 150–160. **[7§2]**

[23] Bouyssou, D. and Vansnick, J. C. (1988) A note on the relationship between utility and value functions. In *Risk, Decision and Rationality*, Munier, B. (ed), D. Reidel, 103–114. **[2§13]**

[24] Bouyssou, D. (1990) Building criteria: a prerequisite for MCDA. In *Readings in MCDA*, Bana e Costa, C. (ed), Springer-Verlag. **[3§1]**

[25] Bouyssou, D. and Perny, P. (1990) Ranking methods for valued preference relations: a characterization of a method based on leaving and entering flows. *Cahier du Lamsade* **101**. Université Paris-Dauphine. **[7§15]**

[26] Bouyssou, D. (1991) Ranking methods based on valued preference relations: a characterization of the net flow method. Submitted for publication. **[7§15]**

[27] Brans, J. P. and Vincke, Ph. (1985) A preference ranking organization method. *Management Science* **31**(6), 647–656. **[5§9]**

[28] Brown, D. (1975) Aggregation of preferences. *Quarterly Journal of Economics* **89**, 456–469. **[7§5]**

[29] Buchanan, J. (1986) Multiple objective mathematical programming: a review. *New Zealand Operational Research* **14**, 1–27. **[7§6]**

[30] Buchanan, J. and Daellenbach, H. (1987) A comparative evaluation of interactive solution methods for multiple objective decision models. *European Journal of Operational Research* **29**, 353–359. **[6§1]**

[31] Buffet, P., Gremy, J., Marc, M. and Sussmann, B. (1967) Peut-on choisir en tenant compte de critères multiples? Une méthode (ELECTRE) et trois applications. *Revue METRA* **VI**(2), 283–316. **[5§2;7§13]**

[32] Chalmet, L., Francis, L. and Kolen, A. (1981) Finding efficient solutions for rectilinear distance location problems efficiently. *European Journal of Operational Research* **6**, 117–124. **[3§13;7§7]**

[33] Chankong, V. and Haimes, Y. (1983) *Multiobjective decision making: theory and methodology*. North-Holland, New York. **[6,7§6]**

[34] Charnes, A. and Cooper, W. (1977) Goal programming and multiple objective optimizations. *European Journal of Operational Research* **1**, 39–54. **[7§6]**

[35] Climaco, J. and Henggeler Antunes, C. (1987) TRIMAP: an interactive tricriteria linear programming package. *Foundations of Control Engineering* **12**(3), 101–119. **[7§2,11]**

[36] Cochrane, J. and Zeleny, M. (eds) (1973) *Multiple Criteria Decision Making*. University of South Carolina Press, Columbia, South Carolina. **[4,5,6]**

[37] Cohen, M., Jaffray, J. Y. and Said, T. (1983) Comparaison expérimentale de comportements individuels dans le risque et dans l'incertain pour des gains et des pertes. *Bulletin de Mathématiques Economiques* **18**, octobre, 17–77. **[2§14]**

[38] Colson, G. (1985) Theories of risk and MCDM. In *MCDM and Applications*, G. Fandel and J. Spronk (eds), Springer-Verlag, 171–196. **[2§14;7§8]**

[39] Colson, G. (1989) MARS: a multiattribute utility ranking support for risk situations, with a P,Q,I,R relational system of preferences. *Mathematical and Computer Modelling* **12**(10), 1269–1298. **[7§11]**

[40] Cox, R., Thomas, J., Revelle, C. and Cohon, J. (1980) Methodologies for multiple objective shortest path problems. ORSA/TIMS Joint National Meeting, Colorado Springs. **[7§7]**

[41] D'Avignon, G. and Vincke, Ph. (1988) An outranking method under uncertainty. *European Journal of Operational Research* **36**, 311–321. **[5§10]**

[42] De Montgolfier, J. and Bertier, P. (1978) *Approche multicritère des problèmes de décision*. Hommes et techniques, Paris. **[5]**

[43] De Samblanckx, S., Depraetere, P. and Muller, H. (1982) Critical considerations concerning the multicriteria analysis by the method of Zionts and Wallenius. *European Journal of Operational Research* **10**(1), 70–76. **[6§6]**

[44] Despontin, M. and Vincke, Ph. (1977) Multiple criteria economic policy. Proceedings of the EURO II congress, North-Holland. **[6§6;7§13]**

[45] Despontin, M., Moscarola, H. and Spronk, J. (1983) A user-oriented listing of MCDM. *Revue Belge de Recherche Opérationnelle, Statistique et Informatique* **23**(4), 3–110. **[7§11]**

[46] Doignon, J. P., Monjardet, B., Roubens, M. and Vincke, Ph. (1986) Biorder families, valued relations and preference modelling. *Journal of Mathematical Psychology* **30**(4), 435–480. **[2]**

[47] Doignon, J. P. (1987) Threshold representations of multiple semiorders. *SIAM Journal on Algebraic and Discrete Methods* **8**, 77–84. **[2§12]**

[48] Doignon, J. P. (1988a) Partial structures of preference. In *Non-conventional preference relations in decision-making*, J. Kacprzyk and M. Roubens (eds), Springer-Verlag, 301, 22–35. **[2§10]**

[49] Doignon, J. P. (1988b) Sur les représentations minimales des semiordres et des ordres d'intervalle. Mathématiques et Sciences Humaines **101**, 49–59. **[2§6]**

[50] Doignon, J. P. and Falmagne, J. C. (1991) Uniqueness in attribute weighting and in representation of qualitative probabilities. In *Mathematical Psychology: current developments*, J. P. Doignon and J. C. Falmagne (eds), Springer-Verlag. **[7§2]**

[51] Drugman, R. (1990) Etude sur la signification pour le décideur des poids dans les méthodes multicritères d'aide à la décision. Dissertation, Université Libre de Bruxelles. **[7§2]**

[52] Dushnik, B. and Miller, E. (1941) Partially ordered sets. *American Journal of Mathematics* **63**, 600–610. **[2§10]**

[53] Dyer, J. (1973) A time-sharing computer program for the solution of the multiple criteria problem. *Management Science* **19**(12), 1379–1383. **[6§3]**

[54] Eckenrode, R. (1966) Weighting multiple criteria. *Management Science* **12**, 180–192. **[7§2]**

[55] Ecker, J., Hegner, N. and Kouada, I. (1980) Generating all maximal efficient faces for multiple objective linear programs. *Journal of Optimization Theory and Applications* **30**, 353–381. **[3§13;7§6]**

[56] Evans, G. (1984) An overview of techniques for solving multiobjective mathematical programs. *Management Science* **30**(11); 1268–1282. **[7§6]**

[57] Evans, J. and Steuer, R. (1973) Generating efficient extreme points in linear multiple objective programming. In *Multiple Criteria Decision Making*, J. Cochrane and M. Zeleny (eds), University of South Carolina Press, Columbia. **[3§13;7§6]**

[58] Fandel, G. and Spronk, J. (eds) (1985) *Multiple criteria decision methods and applications.* Springer-Verlag. **[3,4,5,6]**

[59] Farquhar, P. (1984) Utility assessment methods. *Management Science* **30**(11), 1283–1300. **[4§4]**

[60] Fichefet, J. (1976) GPSTEM: an interactive multiobjective optimization method. In *Progress in O.R.*, A. Prekopa (ed), North-Holland, 317–332. **[7§11]**

[61] Fishburn, P. C. (1967) Methods of estimating additive utilities. *Management Science* **13**(7), 435–453. **[4§4]**

[62] Fishburn, P. C. (1968) Utility theory. *Management Science* **14**, 335–378. **[2,4]**

[63] Fishburn, P. C. (1970a) *Utility theory for decision-making.* Wiley, New York. **[2,4]**

[64] Fishburn, P. C. (1970b) Utility theory with inexact preferences and degrees of preference. *Synthese* **21**, 204–222. **[2]**

[65] Fishburn, P. C. (1970c) Arrow's impossibility theorem: concise proof and infinite voters. *Journal of Economic Theory* **2**, 103–106. **[7§3]**

[66] Fishburn, P. C. (1970d) Intransitive individual indifference and transitive majority. *Econometrica* **38**, 482–489. **[7§3]**

[67] Fishburn, P. C. (1971) The theory of representative majority decision. *Econometrica* **39**, 273–284. **[7§4]**

[68] Fishburn, P. C. (1973) Binary choice probabilities: on the varieties of stochastic transitivity. *Journal of Mathematical Psychology* **10**, 327–352. **[2§12]**

[69] Fishburn, P. C. (1974a) Lexicographic orders, utilities and decision rules: a survey. *Management Science* **20**, 1442–1471. **[7§1]**

[70] Fishburn, P. C. (1974b) On collective rationality and a generalized impossibility theorem. *Review of Economic Studies* **41**, 445–457. **[7§3]**

[71] Fishburn, P. C. (1975) Semiorders and choice functions. *Econometrica* **43**, 975–977. **[7§5]**

[72] Fishburn, P. C. (1976a) Non-compensatory preferences. *Synthese* **33**, 393–403. **[7§2]**

[73] Fishburn, P. C. (1976b) Representable choice functions. *Econometrica* **44**, 1033–1043. **[7§5]**

[74] Fishburn, P. C. (1977) Multicriteria choice functions based on binary relations. *Journal of Operational Research* **25**, 989–1012. **[7§5]**

[75] Fishburn, P. C. (1978) A survey of multiattribute/multicriteria

evaluation theories. In *Multicriteria Problem Solving*, S. Zionts (ed), Springer-Verlag, 155, 181–224. **[4]**

[76] Fishburn, P. C. (1982) *The foundations of expected utility.* D. Reidel. **[2§14]**

[77] Fishburn, P. C. (1985) *Interval orders and interval graphs.* Wiley, New York. **[2]**

[78] Fodor, J. C. (1991) Strict preference relations based on weak *t*-norms, to appear in *Fuzzy Sets and Systems.* **[2§12]**

[79] Gal, T. (1977) A general method for determining the set of all efficient solutions to a linear vector problem. *European Journal of Operational Research* **1**, 307–322. **[3§13;7§6]**

[80] Geoffrion, A. (1968) Proper efficiency and the theory of vector maximization. *Journal of Mathematical Analysis and Applications* **22**, 618–630. **[3§6,13;7§6]**

[81] Geoffrion, A., Dyer, J. and Feinberg, A. (1972) An interactive approach for multi-criterion optimization, with an application to the operation of an academic department. *Management Science* **19**(4), 357–368. **[6§3;7§13]**

[82] Gibbard, A. (1973) Manipulation of voting schemes: a general result. *Econometrica* **41**, 587–601. **[7§4]**

[83] Goicoechea, A., Hansen, D. and Duckstein, L. (1982) *Multiobjective decision analysis with engineering and business applications.* Wiley, New York. **[7§6,13]**

[84] Golumbic, M. (1980) *Algorithmic graph theory and perfect graphs.* Academic Press, New York. **[2§7,10]**

[85] Hanse, P., Anciaux, M. and Vincke, Ph. (1976) Quasi-kernels of outranking relations. In *Multiple Criteria Decision Making*, H. Thiriez and S. Zionts (eds), Springer-Verlag, 30, 53–63. **[5§2]**

[86] Henig, M. (1990) Value functions, domination cones and proper efficiency in multicriteria optimization. *Mathematical Programming* **46**, 205–217. **[3§6]**

[87] Herzberger, H. (1973) Ordinal preference and rational choice. *Econometrica* **41**, 187–237. **[7§5]**

[88] Huckert, K., Rhode, R., Roglin, O. and Weber, R. (1980) On the interactive solution to a multicriteria scheduling problem. *Zeitschrift fur Operations Research* **24**, 47–60. **[7§7]**

[89] Hugonnard, J. and Roy, B. (1982) Ranking of suburban line extension projects for the Paris metro system by a multicriteria method. *Transportation Research* **16A**, 301–312. **[5§5;7§13]**

[90] Hwang, C. and Masud, A. (1979) *Multiobjective decision making, methods and applications.* Springer-Verlag, Berlin. **[6;7§6,13]**

[91] Ignizio, J. (1984) A note on the multidimensional dual. *European Journal of Operational Research* **17**(1), 116–122. **[7§6]**

[92] Isermann, H. (1978) Duality in M.O.L.P. In *Multicriteria Problem Solving*, S. Zionts (ed), Springer-Verlag, 155, 274–285. **[7§6]**

[93] Jacquet-Lagrèze, E. (1975) How we can use the notion of semiorders to build outranking relations in multicriteria decision making. In Utility, *Subjective Probability Human Decision Making*, D. Wendt and C. Vlek (eds), D. Reidel. **[5]**

[94] Jacquet-Lagrèze, E. (1981) Systèmes de décision et acteurs multiples: contribution à une théorie de l'action pour les sciences des organisations. Thèse d'Etat, Université Paris Dauphine. **[4§5;7§10]**

[95] Jacquet-Lagrèze, E. (1982a) Binary preference indices: a new look on multicriteria aggregation procedures. *European Journal of Operational Research* **10**, 26–32. **[4,5]**

[96] Jacquet-Lagrèze, E. and Siskos, J. (1982b) Assessing a set of additive utility functions for multicriteria decision making, the UTA method. *European Journal of Operational Research* **10**(2), 151–164. **[4§5]**

[97] Jacquet-Lagrèze, E. and Siskos, J. (1983) Méthode de décision multicritère. Editions Hommes et Techniques. **[4;7§13]**

[98] Jacquet-Lagrèze, E. (1984a) PREFCALC: évaluation et décision multicritère. *Revue de l'utilisateur de IBM-PC* **3**, 38–55. **[4§6;7§11]**

[99] Jacquet-Lagrèze, E. and Shakun, M. (1984b) Decision support systems for semistructured buying decisions. *European Journal of Operational Research* **16**(1), 48–56. **[7§12]**

[100] Jacquet-Lagrèze, E., Meziani, R. and Slowinski, R. (1987) MOLP interactive assessment of a piecewise utility function. *European Journal of Operational Research* **31**(3), 350–357. **[6§10]**

[101] Jacquet-Lagrèze, E. (1990) Interactive assessment of preferences using holistic judgments: the Prefcalc system. In *Readings in MCDA*, C. Bana e Costa (ed), Springer-Verlag. **[4§6]**

[102] Jaffray, J. Y. and Cohen, M. (1982) Experimental results on decision making under uncertainty. *Methods of O.R.* **44**, 275–289. **[2§14]**

[103] Jamison, D. and Lau, L. (1973) Semiorders and the theory of choice. *Econometrica* **41**(5), 901–912. **[7§5]**

[104] Janssen, R., Nijkamp, P. and Rietvelt, P. (1990) Qualitative multicriteria methods in the Netherlands. In *Readings in MCDA*, C. Bana e Costa (ed), Springer-Verlag. **[5§6]**

[105] Kacprzyk, J. and Roubens, M. (eds) (1988) *Non-conventional preference relations in decision making*. Lecture Notes in Economics and Mathematical Systems, 301, Springer-Verlag. **[2;7§9]**

[106] Karpak, B. and Zionts, S. (eds) (1989) Multiple criteria decision

making and risk analysis using microcomputers. NATO ASI Series, *Computer and Systems Sciences* F-56. [**3,4,5,6**]

[107] Keeney, R. (1976a) Group preference axiomatization with cardinal utility. *Management Science* 23, 140–145. [**7§3**]

[108] Keeney, R. and Raiffa, H. (1976b) *Decisions with multiple objectives; preferences and value trade-offs.* J. Wiley and Sons. [**4**]

[109] Kersten, G. (1985) NEGO: group decision support systems. *Information and Management* 8(5), 237–246. [**7§10,11**]

[110] Kersten, G. and Szapiro, T. (1986) Generalized approach to modeling negotiations. *European Journal of Operational Research* 26(1), 142–149. [**7§10**]

[111] Kersten, G. and Szpakowicz, S. (1990) Rule-based formalism and preference representation: an extension of negoplan. *European Journal of Operational Research* 45, 309–323. [**7§10**]

[112] Korhonen, P. and Laakso, J. (1986) A visual interactive method for solving the multicriteria problem. *European Journal of Operational Research* 24(2), 277–287. [**6§9**]

[113] Korhonen, P. (1987) VIG: a visual interactive support system for MCDM. *Revue Belge de Recherche Opérationnelle, de Statistique et d'Informatique* 27(1), 3–15. [**7§11**]

[114] Krantz, D., Luce, D., Suppes, P. and Tversky, A. (1971) *Foundations of measurement* 1. Academic Press. [**2,4**]

[115] Kreweras, G. (1976) Les préordres totaux compatibles avec un ordre partiel. *Mathématiques et Sciences Humaines* 53, 5–30. [**2§17;7§3**]

[116] Leberling, H. (1981) On finding compromise solutions in multicriteria problems using the fuzzy min-operator. *Fuzzy Sets and Systems* 6, 105–118. [**7§9**]

[117] Leclercq, J. P. (1982) Stochastic programming: an interactive multicriteria approach. *European Journal of Operational Research* 10, 33–41. [**7§6**]

[118] Leclercq, J. P. (1984) Propositions d'extension de la notion de dominance en présence de relations d'ordre sur les pseudo-critères: MELCHIOR. *Revue Belge de Recherche Opérationnelle, de Statistique et d'Informatique* 24(1), 32–46. [**5§6,7**]

[119] Levine, P. and Pomerol, J. (1986) PRIAM, an interactive program for choosing among multiple attribute alternatives. *European Journal of Operational Research* 25, 272–280. [**7§11,12**]

[120] Lowe, T. (1978) Efficient solutions in multiobjective tree network location problems. *Transportation Science* 12. [**3§13;7§7**]

[121] Lowe, T., Thisse, J., Ward, J. and Wendell, R. (1984) On efficient solutions to multiple objective mathematical programs. *Management Science* 30(11), 1346–1349. [**3§13;7§6**]

[122] Luce, D. (1956) Semiorders and a theory of utility discrimination. *Econometrica* **24**, 178–191. **[2§6]**

[123] Luce, D., Krantz, D., Suppes, P. and Tversky, A. (1990) *Foundations of measurement*, Vol. 3, Academic Press. **[2,4]**

[124] McCord, M. and De Neufville, R. (1982) Empirical demonstrations that expected utility decision analysis is not operational. In *Foundations of utility and risk theory*, B. Stigum and F. Wenstop (eds), D. Reidel. **[2§14]**

[125] Mareschal, B. (1988a) Weight stability intervals in multicriteria decision aid. *European Journal of Operational Research* **33**, 54–64. **[5§9;7§11]**

[126] Mareschal, B. and Brans, J. P. (1988b) Geometrical representations for MCDA. *European Journal of Operational Research* **34**, 69–77. **[5§9;7§11]**

[127] Martins, E. (1984) On a multicriteria shortest path problem. *European Journal of Operational Research* **16**(2), 236–245. **[7§7]**

[128] Matarazzo, B. (1986) Multicriterion analysis of preferences by means of pairwise actions and criterion comparisons (MAPPAC). *Applied Mathematics and Computation* **18**(2), 119–141. **[7§11]**

[129] Matarazzo, B. (1988) Preference ranking global frequencies in multicriterion analysis (PRAGMA). *European Journal of Operational Research* **36**(1), 36–50. **[7§11]**

[130] Monjardet, B. (1973) Tournois et ordres médians pour une opinion. *Mathématiques et Sciences Humaines* **43**, 55–70. **[7§1,3]**

[131] Monjardet, B. (1976) Lhuilier contre Condorcet au pays des paradoxes. *Mathématiques et Sciences Humaines* **54**, 33–43. **[7§4]**

[132] Monjardet, B. (1978a) An axiomatic theory of tournament aggregation. *Mathematics of O.R.*, 334–351. **[7§3]**

[133] Monjardet, B. and Jacquet-Lagrèze, E. (eds) (1978b) Modélisation des préférences et quasi-ordres. *Mathématiques et Sciences Humaines* **62** and **63** (special editions). **[2§6]**

[134] Monjardet, B. (1978c) Axiomatiques et propriétés des quasi-ordres. *Mathématiques et Sciences Humaines* **63**, 51–82. **[2§6]**

[135] Moscarola, J. and Roy, B. (1977) Procédure automatique d'examen de dossiers fondée sur un classement trichotomique en présence de critères multiples. *Revue Française d'Informatique et de Recherche Opérationnelle* **22**, 2. **[5§8;7§11,13]**

[136] Mote, J., Olson, D. and Venkataramanan, M. (1988) A comparative multiobjective programming study. *Mathematical Computer Modelling* **10**(10), 719–729. **[6§1]**

[137] Mousseau, V. (1989) La notion d'importance relative des critères. Dissertation, Université Paris-Dauphine. **[7§2]**

[138] Narula, S. and Weistroffer, H. (1989) Algorithm for multiobjective non linear programming problems: an overview. In *Improving decision making in optimization*, A. Lockett and G. Islei (eds), Lecture Notes in Economics and Mathematical Systems 335, Springer-Verlag, 434–443. **[7§6]**

[139] Orlovsky, S. (1978) Decision-making with a fuzzy preference relation. *Fuzzy Sets and Systems* **1**, 155–167. **[7§9]**

[140] Osborne, D. (1976) Irrelevant alternatives and social welfare. *Econometrica* **44**, 1001–1015. **[7§3]**

[141] Ovchinnikov, S. and Roubens, M. (1991) On fuzzy strict preference, indifference and incomparability relations. To appear in *Fuzzy Sets and Systems*. **[2§12]**

[142] Paelinck, J. (1978) Qualiflex, a flexible multiple criteria method. *Economic letters* **3**, 193–197. **[5§6]**

[143] Pastijn, H. and Leysen, J. (1988) A decision support package for material acquisition and personnel selection. In *Information technology for organisational systems*, H. Bullinger *et al.* (eds), Elsevier. **[7§11]**

[144] Pastijn, H. and Leysen, J. (1989) Constructing an outranking relation with Oreste. *Mathematical and Computer Modelling* **12**(10), 1255–1268. **[5§6]**

[145] Pattanaik, P. (1970) Sufficient conditions for the existence of a choice set under majority voting. *Econometrica* **38**, 165–170. **[4§5]**

[146] Peleg, B. (1978) Consistent voting systems. *Econometrica* **46**, 153–161. **[7§4]**

[147] Philip, J. (1972) Algorithms for the vector maximization problem. *Mathematical Programming* **2**(2), 207–229. **[3§13;7§6]**

[148] Pirlot, M. (1990) Minimal representation of a semiorder. *Theory and Decision* **28**, 109–141. **[2§6]**

[149] Pirlot, M. and Vincke, Ph. (1991) Lexicographic aggregation of semiorders. Submitted for publication. **[7§1]**

[150] Plott, C. (1973) Path independence, rationality and social voting. *Econometrica* **41**, 1075–1091. **[7§5]**

[151] Poincare, H. (1935) *La valeur de la science*. Flammarion. **[2§6]**

[152] Pomerol, J. and Trabelsi, T. (1987) An adaptation of PRIAM to multiobjective linear programming. *European Journal of Operational Research* **31**, 335–341. **[7§12]**

[153] Ribeill, G. (1973) Equilibre, équivalence, ordre et préordre à distance minimum d'un graphe complet. *Mathématiques et Sciences Humaines* **43**, 71–106. **[2§17]**

[154] Rios Insua, D. (1990) *Sensitivity analysis in multiobjective decision making*, Lecture Notes in Economics and Mathematical Systems 347, Springer-Verlag. **[7§6]**

[155] Roberts, F. (1979) Measurement theory. *Encyclopedia of mathematics and its applications* 7, Addison-Wesley. **[2,4]**

[156] Roberts, F. (1985) Applications of the theory of meaningfulness to psychology. *Journal of Mathematical Psychology* 29, 311–332. **[7§2,15]**

[157] Roberts, F. and Rosenbaum, Z. (1986) Scale type, meaningfulness and the possible psychophysical laws. *Mathematical Social Sciences* 12, 77–95. **[7§2,15]**

[158] Rodder, W. (1977) A generalized saddlepoint theory. *European Journal of Operational Research* 1(1), 55–60. **[7§6]**

[159] Romero, C. (1986) A survey of generalized goal programming. *European Journal of Operational Research* 25, 183–191. **[7§6]**

[160] Roubens, M. (1981) Preference relations on actions and criteria in multiple criteria decision making. *European Journal of Operational Research* 10, 51–55. **[5§6]**

[161] Roubens, M. and Vincke, Ph. (1983a) Linear fuzzy graphs. *Fuzzy Sets and Systems* 10, 79–86. **[2§12;7§9]**

[162] Roubens, M. and Vincke, Ph. (1983b) Linear orders and semiorders close to an interval order. *Discrete Applied Mathematics* 6, 311–314. **[2§17]**

[163] Roubens, M. and Vincke, Ph. (1984a) A definition of partial interval orders. In *Trends in Mathematical Psychology*, E. Degreef and J. Van Buggenhaut (eds), North-Holland, 309–316. **[2§10]**

[164] Roubens, M. and Vincke, Ph. (1984b) On families of semiorders and interval orders imbedded in a valued structure of preference: a survey. *Information Sciences* 34, 187–198. **[2§12]**

[165] Roubens, M. and Vincke, Ph. (1985) *Preference modelling*, Springer-Verlag, Lecture Notes in Economics and Mathematical Systems 250. **[2]**

[166] Roubens, M. and Vincke, Ph. (1987) Fuzzy preferences in an optimization perspective. *In Optimization models using fuzzy sets and possibility theory*, K. Kacprzyk and S. Orlovski (eds), D. Reidel, Dordrecht, 77–90. **[2§12;7§9]**

[167] Roubens, M. and Vincke, Ph. (1988) Fuzzy possibility graphs and their applications to ranking fuzzy numbers. In *Nonconventional preference relations in decision making*, J. Kacprzyk and M. Roubens (eds), Lecture Notes in Economics and Mathematical Systems 301, Springer-Verlag, 119–129. **[7§9]**

[168] Roy, B. (1968) Classement et choix en présence de points de vue multiples (la méthode Electre). *Revue Française d'Informatique et de Recherche Opérationnelle* 8, 57–75. **[5§2]**

[169] Roy B, (1971a) Problems and methods with multiple objective functions. *Mathematical Programming* 1, 239–266. **[4,5,6]**

[170] Roy, B. and Bertier, P. (1971b) La méthode ELECTRE II. Working paper 142, SEMA. **[5§3]**

[170] Roy, B. and Bertier, P. (1971b) La méthode ELECTRE II. Working paper 142, SEMA. **[5§3]**

[171] Roy, B. and Bertier, P. (1973) La méthode ELECTRE II, une application au média-planning. In *OR 72*, M. Ross (ed), North-Holland, 291–302. **[5§3;7§13]**

[172] Roy, B. (1974) Critères multiples et modélisation des préférences: l'apport des relations de surclassement. *Revue d'Economie Politique* **1**. **[5§1]**

[173] Roy, B., Brans, J. P. and Vincke, Ph. (1975) Aide à la décision multicritère. *Revue Belge de Statistique, d'Informatique et de Recherche Opérationnelle* **15**, 23–53. **[3,4,5,6]**

[174] Roy, B. (1976) From optimization to multicriteria decision aid: three main operational attitudes. In *Multiple Criteria Decision Making*, H. Thiriez and S. Zionts (eds), Springer-Verlag 130, 1–32. **[6§4]**

[175] Roy, B. (1978) ELECTRE III: algorithme de classement basé sur une représentation floue des préférences en présence de critères multiples. *Cahiers du CERO* **20**(1), 3–24. **[5§4]**.

[176] Roy, B. (1981a) A multicriteria analysis for trichotomic segmentation problems. In *Multiple Criteria Analysis*, P. Nijkamp and J. Spronk (eds), Gaver, 245–257. **[5§8]**

[177] Roy, B. and Vincke, Ph. (1981b) Multicriteria analysis: survey and new directions. *European Journal of Operational Research* **8**, 207–218. **[3,4,5,6]**

[178] Roy, B. and Skalka, J. M. (1984a) Electre IS – Aspects méthodologiques et guide d'utilisation. *Document du Lamsade* **30**, Université Paris-Dauphine. **[5§2;7§11]**

[179] Roy, B. and Vincke, Ph. (1984b) Relational systems of preference with one or more pseudo-criteria: some new concepts and results. *Management Science* **30**(11), 1323–1335. **[2§9]**

[180] Roy, B. (1985) *Méthodologie multicritère d'aide à la décision*. Economica, Paris. **[1,2,3]**

[181] Roy, B. and Vincke, Ph. (1987a) Pseudo-orders: definition, properties and numerical representation. *Mathematical Social Sciences* **14**(2), 263–274. **[2§9]**

[182] Roy, B. and Bouyssou, D. (1987b) Famille de critères: problème de cohérence et de dépendance. *Document du Lamsade* **37**, Université Paris-Dauphine. **[3§1;7§2]**

[183] Roy, B. and Bouyssou, D. (1987c) Conflits entre critères et procédures élémentaires d'agrégation multicritère. *Document du Lamsade* **41**, Université Paris-Dauphine. **[7§1,3]**

[184] Roy, B. and Bouyssou, D. (1987d) Procédures d'agrégation multicritère conduisant à un critère unique de synthèse. *Document du Lamsade* **42**, Université Paris-Dauphine. **[4]**

[185] Roy, B. (1989) The outranking approach and the foundations of Electre methods. *Document du Lamsade* **53**, Université Paris-Dauphine (also in Bana e Costa, 1990). **[5§1]**

[186] Roy, B. (1990a) Decision-aid and decision-making. *European Journal of Operational Research* **45**, 324–331 (also in Bana e Costa, 1990). **[3§4]**

[187] Roy, B. (1990b) Sur la notion d'importance relative des critères. 12th Triennal Conference on Operations Research, Athens (Greece). **[7§2]**

[188] Saaty, T. (1980) *The analytic hierarchy process.* McGraw-Hill, New York. **[4§7;7§2,11]**

[189] Sadagopan, S. and Ravindran, A. (1986) Interactive algorithms for multicriteria nonlinear programming problems. *European Journal of Operational Research* **25**, 247–257. **[6§3]**

[190] Sakawa, M. and Yano, H. (1990) Interactive decision-making for multiobjective programming problems with fuzzy parameters. In *Stochastic versus fuzzy approaches to multiobjective mathematical programming under uncertainty*, R. Slowinski and J. Teghem (eds), Kluwer. **[7§9]**

[191] Sawaragi, Y., Nakayama, H. and Tanino, T. (1985) *Theory of multiobjective optimization.* Academic Press, New York. **[7§6]**

[192] Schärlig, A. (1985) *Décider sur plusieurs critères.* Collection Diriger l'Entreprise, Press Polytechniques Romandes. **[4,5,6]**

[193] Sen, A. (1977) Social choice theory: a re-examination. *Econometrica* **45**, 53–90. **[7§3,5]**

[194] Shakun, M. (ed) (1987) *Evolutionary systems design: policy making under complexity and group decision support systems.* Holden-Day, Oakland. **[7§10]**

[195] Simon, H. (1987) Two heads are better than one: the collaboration between AI and OR. *Interfaces* **17**, 8–15. **[7§14]**

[196] Siskos, J., Winkels, H. and Wascher, G. (1983) A bibliography on outranking approaches. *Cahier du Lamsade* **45**, Université Paris-Dauphine. **[5;7§13]**

[197] Skalka, J. M., Bouyssou, D. and Bernabeu, Y. (1984) ELECTRE III et IV: aspects méthodologiques et guide d'utilisation. *Document du Lamsade* **25**, Université Paris-Dauphine. **[5§4,5;7§11]**

[198] Slowinski, R. (1981) Multiobjective network scheduling with efficient use of renewable and nonrenewable resources. *European Journal of Operational Research* **7**, 265–273. **[7§7]**

[199] Slowinski, R. (1986) A multicriteria fuzzy linear programming method for water supply system development planning. *Fuzzy Sets and Systems* **19**, 217–235. [7§9]

[200] Slowinski, R. and Teghem, J. (eds) (1990) *Stochastic versus fuzzy approaches to multiobjective mathematical programming under uncertainty.* Kluwer. [7§6]

[201] Spronk, J. (1981) *Interactive multiple goal programming.* Marinus Nijhoff, The Hague. [7§6,11]

[202] Stancu-Minasian, I. (1984) *Stochastic programming with multiple objective functions.* D. Reidel. [7§6]

[203] Stancu-Minasian, I. (1990) Overview of different approaches for solving stochastic programming problems with multiple objective functions. In *Stochastic versus fuzzy approaches to multiobjective mathematical programming under uncertainty*, R. Slowinski and J. Teghem, (eds), Kluwer. [7§6]

[204] Steuer, R. and Harris, F. (1980) Intra-set point generation and filtering in decision and criterion space. *Computers and Operations Research* **7**, 41–53. [6§8]

[205] Steuer, R. and Choo, E. (1983) An interactive weighted Tchebycheff procedure for multiple objective programming. *Mathematical Programming* **26**, 326–344. [6§8]

[206] Steuer, R. (1986) *Multiple criteria optimization: theory, computation and application.* Wiley, New York. [3;4;7§6,11,13]

[207] Steuer, R. and Gardiner, L. (1990) Interactive multiple objective programming: concepts, current status and future directions. In *Readings in multiple criteria decision-aid*, Bana e Costa (ed), Springer-Verlag. [6§1]

[208] Suppes, P., Krantz, D., Luce, D. and Tversky, A. (1989) *Foundations of measurement*, Vol. 2. Academic Press. [2,4]

[209] Szpilrajn, E. (1930) Sur l'extension de l'ordre partiel. *Fundamenta Mathematicae* **16**. [2§10]

[210] Teghem, J., Dufrane, D., Thauvoye, M. and Kunsch, P. (1986a) STRANGE: an interactive method for multi-objective linear programming under uncertainty. *European Journal of Operational Research* **26**(1), 65–82. [7§6,11]

[211] Teghem, J. and Kunsch, P. (1986b) Interactive methods for multiobjective integer linear programming. In *Large-scale modelling and interactive decision analysis*, G. Fandel *et al.* (eds), Springer-Verlag **273**, 75–87. [6§1;7§6]

[212] Van Wassenhove, L. and Gelders, L. (1980) Solving a bicriterion scheduling problem. *European Journal of Operational Research* **4**, 42–48. [7§7]

[213] Vanderpooten, D. (1988) A multicriteria interactive procedure supporting a directed learning of preferences. Presented at the EURO IX Conference, Paris. [6§11]

[214] Vanderpooten, D. and Vincke, Ph. (1989) Description and analysis of some representative interactive multicriteria procedures. *Mathematical and Computer Modelling* 12(10), 1221–1238. [6]

[215] Vanderpooten, D. (1989) The interactive approach in MCDA: a technical framework and some basic conceptions. *Mathematical and Computer Modelling* 12(10), 1213–1220. [6§12]

[216] Vanderpooten, D. (1990a) Multiobjective programming: basic concepts and approaches. In *Stochastic versus fuzzy approaches to multiobjective mathematical programming under uncertainty*, R. Slowinski and J. Teghem (eds), Kluwer. [7§6]

[217] Vanderpooten, D. (1990b) The construction of prescriptions in outranking methods. In *Readings in MCDA*, C. Bana e Costa (ed), Springer-Verlag. [5§1]

[218] Vansnick, J. C. (1986a) De Borda et Condorcet à l'agrégation multicritère. *Cahier du Lamsade* 70, Univesité Paris-Dauphine. [7§1,2,4]

[219] Vansnick, J. C. (1986b) On the problem of weights in multiple criteria decision making. *European Journal of Operational Research* 24, 288–294. [7§2]

[220] Vincke, Ph. (1974) Problèmes multicritères. *Cahiers du CERO* 16(4), 41–50. [3§13;7§7]

[221] Vincke, Ph. (1976a) Modélisation des préférences et théorie de l'utilité: résultats existants et voies de recherche. *Revue Belge de Recherche Opérationnelle, de Statistique et d'Informatique* 16(4), 1–16. [2,4]

[222] Vincke, Ph. (1976b) Une méthode interactive en programmation linéaire à plusieurs fonctions économiques. *Revue Française d'Informatique et de Recherche Opérationnelle* 2, 5–20. [6§6]

[223] Vincke, Ph. (1977) Quasi-kernels of minimum weakness in a graph. *Discrete Mathematics* 20, 187–192. [5§2]

[224] Vincke, Ph. (1978a) Quasi-ordres généralisés et représentation numérique. *Mathématiques et Sciences Humaines* 62, 35–60. [2§6]

[225] Vincke, Ph. (1978b) Ordres et Préordres totaux à distance minimum d'un quasi-ordre. *Cahiers du CERO* 20(3), 451–462. [2§17]

[226] Vincke, Ph. (1980a) Linear utility functions on semiordered mixture spaces. *Econometrica* 48(3), 771–776. [2§6]

[227] Vincke, Ph. (1980b) Vrais, quasi, pseudo et précritères dans un ensemble fini: propriétés et algorithmes. *Cahier du Lamsade* 27, Université Paris-Dauphine. [2]

[228] Vincke, Ph. (1981) Preference modelling: a survey and an

experiment. In *Operational Research* **81**, J. P. Brans (ed), North-Holland, 341–354. [2§18]

[229] Vincke, Ph. (1982a) Présentation et analyse de neuf méthodes multicritères interactives. *Cahier du Lamsade* **42**, Université Paris-Dauphine. [6]

[230] Vincke, Ph. (1982b) Arrow's theorem is not a surprising result. *European Journal of Operational Research* **10**, 22–25. [7§3]

[231] Vincke, Ph. (1982c) Aggregation of preferences: a review. *European Journal of Operational Research* **9**, 17–22. [7§3,4,5]

[232] Vincke, Ph. (1983) Problèmes de localisation multicritères. *Cahiers du CERO* **25**(3), 333–338. [7§7]

[233] Vincke, Ph. (1986) Analysis of multicriteria decision aid in Europe. Invited Review, *European Journal of Operational Research* **25**, 160–168. [4,5,6]

[234] Vincke, Ph. (1988) (P,Q,I)-preference structures. In *Non-conventional preference relations in decision making*, J. Kacprzyk and M. Roubens (eds), Springer-Verlag 301, 72–81. [2§9]

[235] Vincke, Ph. (1989) *L'aide multicritère à la décision*. Editions de l'Université de Bruxelles et Editions Ellipses. [All]

[236] Vincke, Ph. (1991) Exploitation d'une relation non valuée dans une problématique de rangement complet. *Document du Lamsade* **62**, Université Paris-Dauphine. [7§15]

[237] Von Neumann, J. and Morgenstern, O. (1967) *Theory of games and economic behaviour*. Princeton University Press, 3rd edn. [2§14]

[238] Wendel, R. (1980) Multiple objective mathematical programming with respect to multiple decision makers. *Operational Research* **28**(5), 1100–1111. [7§10]

[239] White, D. (1983) A selection of multiobjective interactive programming methods. In *Multiobjective decision making*, S. French, G. Hartley, M. Thomas and D. White (eds), Academic Press, London, 99–126. [6§1]

[240] Wierzbicki, A. (1980) The use of reference objectives in multiobjective optimization. In *MCDM Theory and Application*, G. Fandel and T. Gal (eds), Springer-Verlag 177, 468–486. [6§7]

[241] Wierzbicki, A. (1982) A mathematical basis for satisficing decision making. *Mathematical Modelling* **3**, 391–405. [6§7]

[242] Weirzbicki, A. (1986) On the completeness and constructiveness of parametric characterizations to vector optimization problems. *OR Spektrum* **8**(2), 73–87. [6§7]

[243] Yu, P. and Zeleny, M. (1975) The set of all nondominated solutions in linear case and a multicriteria simplex method. *Journal of Mathematical Analysis and Applications* **49**, 430–468. [3§13;7§6]